The ROS2 and Python Robotics Playbook

Designing and Controlling Autonomous Robots for Navigation and Real-World Interaction

Thompson Carter

Rafael Sanders

Miguel Farmer

Copyright © 2025

[3]

Contents

Chapter 1: Getting Started — Your First Steps into ROS2 and Python Robotics 23

1.1 Understanding the Power of Robotics 24

1.1.1 Robotics: More Than Meets the Eye 24

1.1.2 Real-World Applications 25

1.1.3 The Key Principles Driving Robotic Innovation 27

1.1.4 Harnessing Robots Safely and Ethically 28

1.2 Why ROS2 and Python? 29

1.2.1 The Power of ROS2 29

1.2.2 The Case for Python in Robotics 32

1.2.3 The Perfect Pair: Why ROS2 + Python is Ideal 33

1.3 Setting Up Your Development Environment (ROS2, Python, and IDEs) 34

1.3.1 Overview of the Process 34

1.3.2 Choosing an Operating System 36

1.3.3 Installing ROS2 37

1.3.4 Installing Python (If Needed) 38

1.3.5 Picking an IDE 39

1.3.6 Validating Your Setup 41

1.4 Key Concepts and Terminology 43

1.4.1 Nodes 43

1.4.2 Topics 44

1.4.3 Messages 44

1.4.4 Services.. 45

1.4.5 Actions 45

1.4.6 Parameter Server 46

1.4.7 Workspaces and Packages 46

1.4.8 Simulation and Visualization Tools 47

1.4.9 Putting It All Together 47

Chapter Summary 48

Key Takeaways:.. 48

What's Next? 49

Chapter 2: Core Concepts of ROS2 51

2.1 Nodes, Topics, Services, and Actions 52

2.1.1 Nodes: The Fundamental Units of Computation 52

2.1.2 Topics: Sharing Data in Real Time (Publish-Subscribe) 53

2.1.3 Services: Synchronous Request-Response 54

2.1.4 Actions: Handling Long-Running Tasks with Feedback.......... 55

2.1.5 Diagram 1: Node Interactions Overview 56

2.2 Packages and Workspaces: Organizing Your Project......57

2.2.1 ROS2 Packages: Bundling Functionality 57

2.2.2 Workspaces: Your Project's Ecosystem 58

2.2.3 Diagram 2: Typical ROS2 Workspace Structure.................... 59

2.2.4 Creating a Package: Step-by-Step 60

2.3 ROS2 Communication Mechanisms...................................61

2.3.1 DDS and Discovery... 61

2.3.2 Quality of Service (QoS) Settings.............................. 62

2.3.3 Diagram 3: ROS2 Communication Under the Hood 63

2.3.4 Multi-Machine Systems 64

2.4 Launch Files and Parameter Servers 64

2.4.1 Launch Files: Automating Node Startup..................... 65

2.4.2 Parameter Servers: Flexible Configuration 66

2.5 Hands-On: Building Your First ROS2 Node in Python .67

2.5.1 Prerequisites.. 67

2.5.2 Step 1: Create a Package 67

2.5.3 Step 2: Write the Publisher Node 68

2.5.4 Step 3: Write the Subscriber Node 70

2.5.5 Step 4: Update setup.py 72

2.5.6 Step 5: Make Scripts Executable.............................. 73

2.5.7 Step 6: Build and Source....................................... 73

2.5.8 Step 7: Run the Nodes 74

2.5.9 Creating a Simple Launch File (Optional).................... 75

Chapter Summary 76

Looking Ahead 78

Chapter 3: Python Fundamentals for Robotics.................. 80

3.1 Python Basics Refresher (for Beginners) 81

3.1.1 Why Python in Robotics? 81

3.1.2 Core Python Syntax and Structures 82

3.1.3 Diagram 1: Python's Basic Building Blocks 86

3.2 Essential Python Libraries for Robotics (NumPy, OpenCV, etc.) 87

3.2.1 NumPy: Numerical Computing at Scale 87

3.2.2 OpenCV: Powerhouse for Computer Vision 88

3.2.3 Matplotlib & Plotly: Visualizing Data 89

3.2.4 SciPy & scikit-learn: Advanced Processing and ML 90

3.2.5 Additional Tools and Libraries 90

3.2.6 Diagram 2: The Python Robotics Ecosystem 91

3.3 Writing Efficient and Clean Python Code 92

3.3.1 Code Readability and Style 92

3.3.2 Optimizing Performance 93

3.3.3 Modular Design and Reusability 94

3.3.4 Concurrency and Parallelism 94

3.4 Debugging and Testing Your Code 95

3.4.1 Debugging Techniques 95

3.4.2 Common Pitfalls 96

3.4.3 Testing Strategies 96

3.4.4 Diagram 3: The Testing Pyramid 98

3.5 Hands-On: Simple Sensor Data Processing with Python 99

3.5.1 Project Overview...99

3.5.2 Step 1: Set Up the Project Structure.............................99

3.5.3 Step 2: Simulate or Import Sensor Data 100

3.5.4 Step 3: Implement a Simple Moving Average Filter 101

3.5.5 Step 4: Detect Outliers 102

3.5.6 Step 5: Real-Time Plotting (Optional) 102

3.5.7 Putting It All Together 105

Chapter Summary 107

Where to Go from Here? 109

Chapter 4: Sensors, Perception, and Environment Mapping 110

4.1 Introduction to Common Robotics Sensors (LIDAR, Sonar, Cameras, IMUs)..111

4.1.1 Why Sensors Are the Robot's "Eyes and Ears" 111

4.1.2 LIDAR 112

4.1.3 Sonar 112

4.1.4 Cameras 113

4.1.5 IMUs 114

4.1.6 Diagram 1: Typical Sensor Placement on a Mobile Robot ... 115

4.2 Data Collection and Processing with ROS2 Topics 116

4.2.1 ROS2 Topics Recap...116

4.2.2 Common ROS2 Message Types for Sensors 116

4.2.3 Basic Workflow for Sensor Data in ROS2......................117

4.2.4 Transform Frames (tf2) 118

4.3 Building a Simple SLAM (Simultaneous Localization and Mapping) System 119

4.3.1 The Essence of SLAM 119

4.3.2 Popular SLAM Algorithms 120

4.3.3 Setting Up a Basic LIDAR SLAM in ROS2 121

4.3.4 Key SLAM Challenges 123

4.4 Visualizing Sensor Data in RViz 123

4.4.1 Why Use RViz? 123

4.4.2 Basic RViz Setup 124

4.4.3 Common Displays and Their Uses 124

4.5 Hands-On: Creating an Obstacle-Aware Robot Simulation 126

4.5.1 Project Overview 126

4.5.2 Step 1: Install or Confirm Your Simulator 127

4.5.3 Step 2: Create a Robot Description 127

4.5.4 Step 3: Launch the Simulation 128

4.5.5 Step 4: SLAM Integration 130

4.5.6 Step 5: Teleoperate the Robot 132

4.5.7 Step 6: Visualize in RViz 132

4.5.8 Extending the Project 133

Chapter Summary 133

Where to Go Next.. 134

Chapter 5: Kinematics, Control, and Navigation 136

5.1 Robot Kinematics: Differential Drive, Ackermann

Steering, and More 137

    5.1.1 What Is Kinematics? 137

    5.1.2 Differential Drive Kinematics 137

    5.1.3 Ackermann Steering 139

    5.1.4 Holonomic and Omni-Directional Drives 140

    5.1.5 Diagram 1: Common Drive Configurations 141

5.2 PID Control and Advanced Control Algorithms 144

    5.2.1 The PID Controller... 144

    5.2.2 Limitations of Basic PID 145

    5.2.3 Advanced Control: LQR, MPC, and Beyond 146

    5.2.4 Practical Considerations 147

5.3 Motion Planning and Path Tracking in ROS2 147

    5.3.1 The ROS2 Navigation Stack (nav2) 148

    5.3.2 Global vs. Local Planning... 148

    5.3.3 Path Tracking.. 149

    5.3.4 Diagram 2: Simplified ROS2 Navigation Stack............. 150

5.4 Navigating in Dynamic Environments 151

    5.4.1 The Complexity of Dynamic Obstacles.......................... 151

    5.4.2 Strategies for Dynamic Navigation 152

5.4.3 Sensor Fusion 152

5.4.4 Diagram 3: Dynamic Environment Navigation Flow 153

5.5 Hands-On: Autonomous Navigation in a Simulated

Indoor Environment 153

5.5.1 Project Overview 154

5.5.2 Step 1: Create an Indoor World 154

5.5.3 Step 2: Configure Your Robot 155

5.5.4 Step 3: Set Up nav2 156

5.5.5 Step 4: Launch Everything and Provide a Goal 158

5.5.6 Step 5: Testing and Troubleshooting 159

5.5.7 Extension: Dynamic Behavior 160

Chapter Summary 160

What's Next? 162

Chapter 6: Real-World Robot Building and Integration .. 164

6.1 Choosing Motors, Motor Drivers, and Power Systems .165

6.1.1 Motor Selection: DC, Stepper, or Brushless? 165

6.1.2 Understanding Gearboxes and Torque Requirements 166

6.1.3 Motor Drivers and ESCs 167

6.1.4 Power Systems: Batteries and Voltage Regulation 171

6.2 Mechanical Design Considerations 173

6.2.1 Chassis Materials and Construction 173

6.2.2 Weight Distribution and Center of Gravity 174

[11]

6.2.3 Shock Absorption and Durability 174

6.2.4 Diagram 2: Basic Robot Chassis Layout 175

6.3 Wiring and Hardware Setup for ROS2 Compatibility ..176

6.3.1 Choosing a Single-Board Computer or Microcontroller 176

6.3.2 Communication Interfaces 177

6.3.3 Power Wiring Basics 177

6.3.4 ROS2 Integration 178

6.4 Integrating Sensors (LIDAR, Ultrasonic, Camera) on a Physical Robot 179

6.4.1 LIDAR Setup 179

6.4.2 Ultrasonic Sensors 180

6.4.3 Cameras 180

6.4.4 Combining Sensor Outputs 181

6.5 Hands-On: Assembling a Small Autonomous Mobile Robot 181

6.5.1 Materials and Tools 182

6.5.2 Step 1: Physical Assembly of the Chassis 183

6.5.3 Step 2: Mounting Electronics and Battery 183

6.5.4 Step 3: Wiring and Connectivity 186

6.5.5 Step 4: ROS2 Setup on the Raspberry Pi 187

6.5.6 Step 5: Motor Control Node and Odometry 188

6.5.7 Step 6: LIDAR Node and Basic Obstacle Avoidance 188

6.5.8 Step 7: Testing and Calibration 189

6.5.9 Step 8: Expanding Capabilities 190

Chapter Summary 190

Where to Go from Here? 192

Chapter 7: Advanced Topics in Autonomous Systems.... 194

7.1 Multi-Robot Communication and Coordination 195

7.1.1 The Rationale for Multi-Robot Systems 195

7.1.2 Communication Infrastructures 195

7.1.3 Coordination Strategies 196

7.1.4 Diagram 1: Multi-Robot Communication Framework 197

7.2 Fleet Management in Warehouses and Industrial Settings
....198

7.2.1 The Rise of Robotic Fleets 198

7.2.2 Fleet Management Components 198

7.2.3 Key Algorithms and Approaches 200

7.2.4 Safety and Human-Robot Interaction 200

7.3 Machine Learning and Computer Vision Applications .201

7.3.1 The Power of ML in Robotics 201

7.3.2 Convolutional Neural Networks (CNNs) 201

7.3.3 Reinforcement Learning (RL) 202

7.3.4 Real-Time Constraints 202

7.4 Edge Computing and Cloud Integration 203

7.4.1 Edge vs. Cloud: A Balancing Act 203

7.4.2 Why Edge Computing? 203

7.4.3 Why Cloud Integration? 204

7.4.4 Hybrid Architecture 204

7.5 Hands-On: Implementing a Simple Object Detection
Pipeline with Python 205

7.5.1 Project Overview 206

7.5.2 Step 1: Install Required Libraries 206

7.5.3 Step 2: Download a Pre-Trained Model 206

7.5.4 Step 3: Image Preprocessing 207

7.5.5 Step 4: Inference and Post-Processing 208

7.5.6 Step 5: Visualize Results 209

7.5.7 Step 6: Putting It All Together 210

7.5.8 Testing the Pipeline 213

7.5.9 Scaling to Real-Time Robotics 214

Chapter Summary 215

Where to Go Next? 216

Chapter 8: Building Robots for Space Exploration —
Advanced Robotic Systems 218

8.1 Unique Challenges in Space Robotics (Extreme
Environments, Latency, Reliability) 219

8.1.1 Extreme Environments: Harsh Conditions Beyond Earth 219

8.1.2 High Communication Latency 220

8.1.3 Reliability and Redundancy......................................221

8.1.4 Diagram 1: Space Robot Environment Challenges...............222

8.2 Advanced Navigation: Combining Traditional and AI-Based Approaches..223

8.2.1 Classical Robotics Navigation.................................223

8.2.2 AI-Driven Navigation 223

8.2.3 Hybrid Approaches 224

8.3 Teleoperation vs. Full Autonomy for Extraterrestrial Missions...225

8.3.1 Teleoperation: When Humans Pull the Strings...................225

8.3.2 Full Autonomy: Necessity for Deep Space......................225

8.3.3 Partial Autonomy: A Balanced Approach........................226

8.4 Future Trends: Swarm Robotics, In-Situ Resource Utilization, and More 226

8.4.1 Swarm Robotics 226

8.4.2 In-Situ Resource Utilization (ISRU) 227

8.4.3 Off-World Factories and Autonomous Mining 227

8.4.4 Diagram 2: Future Space Robotics Scenarios 228

8.5 Hands-On: Simulating a Rover Mission in a Martian-Like ROS2 Environment...229

8.5.1 Project Overview..229

8.5.2 Step 1: Setting Up the Simulation World.....................230

8.5.3 Step 2: Configuring the Rover 231

8.5.4 Step 3: Basic Navigation and Autonomy 233

8.5.5 Step 4: Introducing Communication Delay (Optional) 234

8.5.6 Step 5: Testing Your Martian Rover 235

8.5.7 Step 6: Extending the Simulation 236

Chapter Summary 237

Where to Go Next? 239

Chapter 9: Troubleshooting, Testing, and Continuous
Improvement 241

9.1 Common Issues and Debugging Techniques in ROS2 .242

9.1.1 Why Debugging Matters 242

9.1.2 Common ROS2 Pitfalls.. 242

9.1.3 Debugging Techniques and Tools 244

9.2 Testing Methodologies: Unit Tests, Integration Tests, and
Simulations 246

9.2.1 Why Test? 246

9.2.2 Unit Tests... 246

9.2.3 Integration Tests 247

9.2.4 Simulation Tests 247

9.2.5 Combining All Three 248

9.2.6 Diagram 1: The Testing Pyramid for Robotics 249

9.3 Performance Optimization for Real-Time Systems 250

9.3.1 The Importance of Speed and Timing............................ 250

9.3.2 Profiling and Bottleneck Identification 250

9.3.3 Real-Time Operating Systems (RTOS) and Scheduling 251

9.3.4 Memory and Network Considerations 251

9.3.5 System Architecture Optimization 251

9.4 Documenting and Sharing Your Projects 252

9.4.1 Why Documentation Is Essential 252

9.4.2 Documentation Best Practices 252

9.4.3 Sharing and Collaboration..................... 253

9.4.4 Ensuring Longevity 254

9.5 Hands-On: Creating a Robust Testing Pipeline with ROS2 Tools 254

9.5.1 Project Overview..................... 254

9.5.2 Step 1: Setting Up the Package and Source Code.................. 255

9.5.3 Step 2: Writing Unit Tests 256

9.5.4 Step 3: Writing Integration Tests with ROS2 Launch 257

9.5.5 Step 4: Simulation Test in Gazebo 259

9.5.6 Step 5: One Command to Run All Tests 261

9.5.7 Observing Results and Improving..................... 261

Chapter Summary 262

Where to Go from Here? 264

Chapter 10: Case Studies and Practical Applications 266

10.1 ROS2 in Healthcare: Assistive Robots 267

[17]

10.1.1 Why Healthcare Needs Robotics 267

10.1.2 Example: ROS2-Driven Hospital Delivery Robot 267

10.1.3 Key ROS2 Features for Healthcare 268

10.2 ROS2 in Manufacturing: Automation and Production Lines...271

10.2.1 Evolution of Automation... 271

10.2.2 Case Study: Robot Arm Assembly Line with Real-Time Control 271

10.2.3 Common Patterns in Manufacturing with ROS2 272

10.3 ROS2 in Logistics: Warehouse AGVs (Automated Guided Vehicles)..274

10.3.1 The Rise of AGVs and AMRs 274

10.3.2 Case Study: Large E-Commerce Warehouse....................... 274

10.3.3 ROS2 Advantages in Logistics 275

10.3.4 Integration with WMS (Warehouse Management Systems) 276

10.4 Emerging Use Cases (Agriculture, Search-and-Rescue, and More)..276

10.4.1 Agriculture 276

10.4.2 Search-and-Rescue... 277

10.4.3 Other Emerging Applications 277

10.5 Hands-On: Recreating a Mini Case Study for a Warehouse AGV 279

10.5.1 Project Overview 279

10.5.2 Step 1: Setting Up the Simulated Warehouse 279

10.5.3 Step 2: Configuring Your AGV 281

10.5.4 Step 3: Setting Up nav2 (Navigation Stack) 282

10.5.5 Step 4: Task Manager Node 283

10.5.6 Step 5: Running the Scenario 284

10.5.7 Possible Enhancements 285

Chapter Summary 286

Where to Go from Here? 287

Chapter 11: Looking Ahead — Robotics Trends and Ongoing Innovation 289

11.1 The Future of ROS2: Ecosystem Growth and Support 290

11.1.1 Ongoing Development: A Vibrant Community 290

11.1.2 New Frontiers: WebAssembly, Micro-ROS, and More 291

11.1.3 Growing Industry Adoption 292

11.2 Artificial Intelligence and Robotics: Next-Generation Autonomy 292

11.2.1 The AI-Robotics Convergence 292

11.2.2 Machine Learning Methods Shaping Robotics 293

11.2.3 Pushing Boundaries: Human-Robot Collaboration 293

11.3 Ethical and Societal Considerations in Robotics 294

11.3.1 The Dual-Edged Sword of Automation 294

11.3.2 Safety and Accountability 295

11.3.3 Human-Robot Interaction (HRI)... 295

11.3.4 Fostering Responsible Innovation... 296

11.4.1 Conclusion: The Endless Frontier... 296

11.4.2 Further Resources 297

11.4.3 Lifelong Learning 297

11.5 Hands-On: Setting Up Your Personal Robotics Roadmap 298

11.5.1 Step 1: Identify Your Goals.. 298

11.5.2 Step 2: Assess Current Skills 299

11.5.3 Step 3: Research and Resource Collection........................... 300

11.5.4 Step 4: Create a Timeline... 300

11.5.5 Step 5: Document Progress and Reflect 301

11.5.6 Step 6: Community and Mentors... 301

Chapter Summary 302

A Final Word.. 303

Appendices 305
Appendix A: Glossary of Robotics and ROS2 Terms.........305

A.1 Action 305

A.2 Actuator 306

A.3 Autonomy 306

A.4 Behavior Tree 306

A.5 Costmap 307

A.6 DDS (Data Distribution Service) 307

A.7 Differential Drive 307

A.8 Domain ID.. 307

A.9 Frame (tf2) 308

A.10 Holonomic Drive.. 308

A.11 IMU (Inertial Measurement Unit) 308

A.12 Launch File 308

A.13 Navigation Stack (nav2) 309

A.14 Node... 309

A.15 Parameter 309

A.16 Publish/Subscribe 310

A.17 QoS (Quality of Service)... 310

A.18 Service 310

A.19 SLAM (Simultaneous Localization and Mapping) 310

A.20 TF Tree.. 311

Appendix B: Additional Python Resources and Tutorials ..311

B.1 Official Python Documentation 311

B.2 Python for Robotics Tutorials 312

ROS2 Python Tutorials 312

Appendix C: Recommended Tools, Libraries, and Hardware
Vendors...313

C.1 Development Boards and Single-Board Computers (SBCs) ... 313

C.2 Sensors and Actuators 314

C.3 Libraries for Robotics 315

C.4 Robotics Kits and Chassis Vendors.......................... 316

Appendix D: Troubleshooting Reference Cheat Sheets 316

D.1 ROS2 CLI Commands (Minimal Crash Course) 317

D.3 Parameter Quick Reference.................................... 318

D.4 RViz Visualization Hints 318

D.5 Gazebo Simulation Gotchas.................................... 319

D.6 "What Next?" If All Else Fails................................ 319

Chapter Summary 320

How to Scan a Barcode to Get a Repository

1. **Install a QR/Barcode Scanner** – Ensure you have a barcode or QR code scanner app installed on your smartphone or use a built-in scanner in **GitHub, GitLab, or Bitbucket.**

2. **Open the Scanner** – Launch the scanner app and grant necessary camera permissions.

3. **Scan the Barcode** – Align the barcode within the scanning frame. The scanner will automatically detect and process it.

4. **Follow the Link** – The scanned result will display a **URL to the repository.** Tap the link to open it in your web browser or Git client.

5. **Clone the Repository** – Use **Git clone** with the provided URL to download the repository to your local machine.

Chapter 1: Getting Started — Your First Steps into ROS2 and Python Robotics

Robots capture the imagination like few other technologies. They promise assistance with everyday tasks, tirelessly perform industrial operations, and even venture where humans dare not go—deep under oceans or far beyond Earth's atmosphere. Yet the world of robotics often appears intimidating from the outside. It's easy to assume you need an advanced engineering degree or a massive research budget to build your first functional robot.

Fortunately, that's not the case. Modern frameworks like **ROS2** (Robot Operating System 2) have democratized robotics, making it far more approachable than it once was. Paired with the **Python** programming language—renowned for its simplicity and power—ROS2 can help newcomers and experienced technologists alike design, simulate, and deploy cutting-edge robotic systems. This chapter lays the foundation for your robotics journey, showing you why ROS2 and Python form an ideal pair and how you can set up your development environment to begin experimenting. Along the way, you'll learn the key concepts and terminology that form the bedrock of modern robotics.

Let's embark on a detailed, step-by-step exploration of exactly what's possible, why it matters, and how to get started—no complicated jargon, just straightforward explanations and practical advice.

1.1 Understanding the Power of Robotics

1.1.1 Robotics: More Than Meets the Eye

When people think about **robots**, they often picture humanoid machines, like the ones in science fiction movies. These fictional portrayals can be entertaining but might overshadow the real marvels of robotics. In the real world, robots come in many forms—some are **wheeled platforms** scurrying around factories to move goods from one station to another, others are **surgical arms** assisting doctors in delicate medical procedures, and some are **planetary rovers** collecting soil samples on Mars.

Yet all these variants share a core trait: **they combine sensing, decision-making, and action** into an integrated system. A typical robot will gather information about its environment (through sensors), process that data to make sense of it (often via algorithms or machine learning), and then perform a task or motion (using motors or actuators). This triad—**sense, think, act**—is central to understanding robotics at any level.

Rhetorical Question: Can you imagine a future where robots help with your daily chores, autonomously manage complex industrial processes, and even explore extraterrestrial worlds on our behalf? If that vision excites you, you're in the right place!

1.1.2 Real-World Applications

Robotics has already transformed countless industries, and its influence is only expanding. Consider:

1. **Manufacturing and Logistics**: Robotic arms assemble cars with millimeter precision, while automated guided vehicles (AGVs) navigate warehouse aisles to pick items for shipping. Companies like Amazon, DHL, and major automobile manufacturers depend on

robots to speed up tasks, reduce errors, and maintain consistent quality.

2. **Healthcare and Surgery:** Surgical robots, such as those used for delicate procedures (e.g., heart valve repair), allow doctors to operate with greater precision. Some hospitals also use autonomous disinfecting robots in wards, reducing infection risks.

3. **Agriculture:** Specialized robots can weed large fields without chemicals or precisely harvest crops, improving yield and lowering environmental impact. Sensor-equipped drones monitor crop health from above, guiding farmers to optimize water usage or fertilizer application.

4. **Search and Rescue:** In disaster situations, robots can venture into collapsed buildings or contaminated areas, searching for survivors while keeping humans out of harm's way.

5. **Exploration and Research:** NASA's rovers, such as Perseverance and Curiosity on Mars, gather data about the Martian surface, climate, and geology. These

rugged robots handle extreme environments that are unsafe for humans.

Each of these examples showcases the versatility of robots—they can be **mobile or stationary, small or large, simple or highly complex.** What unifies them is their capacity to operate autonomously (to varying degrees) based on instructions or programmed logic.

1.1.3 The Key Principles Driving Robotic Innovation

Robotics thrives on three overarching principles:

1. **Mechatronics**: The blend of mechanics, electronics, and computer engineering. A single robot might contain an onboard computer (controller), electric motors (actuators), cameras or lasers (sensors), and a mechanical chassis that ties everything together.

2. **Intelligence**: The ability to interpret sensor data and make decisions, typically via algorithms. Basic systems might follow simple rule-based logic (e.g., "If obstacle is detected, turn left"); advanced ones incorporate deep learning for object recognition, or sophisticated planning algorithms to navigate complex maps.

3. **Modularity:** Modern robots are often modular, meaning different components can be replaced or upgraded without redesigning the entire system. Think of a multi-armed robot where each arm runs its own processes, or a drone that can swap out different sensor payloads.

*Analogy: Imagine building with **LEGO** blocks. You can rearrange blocks or add new ones to create different shapes and functions. Similarly, modularity in robotics lets you experiment and innovate more rapidly.*

1.1.4 Harnessing Robots Safely and Ethically

The promise of robotics also raises questions about safety, job displacement, and data privacy. **Collaborative robots** (or "cobots"), designed to work alongside humans without safety cages, must rigorously ensure they do not injure their human colleagues. Additionally, some tasks once done by human labor may become fully automated, impacting local workforces. Researchers and engineers grapple with these ethical implications, trying to build technology that augments human capabilities rather than simply replacing them.

Clarity: We will not delve deeply into the ethics debate in this book, but it's essential to remain mindful of the societal impacts your creations could have. Responsible innovation benefits everyone.

1.2 Why ROS2 and Python?

1.2.1 The Power of ROS2

ROS2, short for **Robot Operating System 2**, is an open-source framework that offers standardized tools, libraries, and conventions for building robot applications. Despite its name, ROS2 is not an actual operating system like Windows or Linux; rather, it runs **on top** of traditional operating systems, providing a **communication layer** and robust environment in which robotic components can work together.

Why Choose ROS2 Over ROS1?

You might have heard of ROS1 (the first major version). ROS2 addresses limitations in ROS1, making it more suitable for commercial and industrial deployments. Notable improvements include:

1. **Cross-Platform Support**: ROS2 runs reliably on Windows, Linux, and macOS, broadening collaboration options.

2. **Real-Time Capabilities**: Industrial robots often require strict timing guarantees. ROS2 is designed with real-time performance in mind.

3. **Enhanced Security**: ROS2 includes improved security features like authentication and encryption.

4. **Distributed System Architecture**: ROS2 uses the Data Distribution Service (DDS) for peer-to-peer discovery and communication, removing the single-point-of-failure "master node" concept from ROS1.

Diagram 1: *ROS2 Communication Flow*

```
+----------------------------------+
|            NETWORK               |
|   (DDS peer-to-peer links)       |
+----------------+-----------------+
                 |
                 |
+----------------------------------+
|     Raspberry Pi (Sensor Node)   |
|                                  |
|   +--------------------------+   /
|   |        Sensor Node       |  |
|   +------------+-------------+   /
|                |                 |
|                |                 |
|<---- Peer-to-Peer DDS -------->| (Discovery &
|                |                 |  data exchange)
+----------------+-----------------+
                 |
                 |
+----------------------------------+
|      Laptop (Control Node)       |
|                                  |
|   +--------------------------+   /
|   |      Control Node        |  |
|   +------------+-------------+   /
|                |                 |
|<---- Peer-to-Peer DDS -------->/
|                |                 |
+----------------+-----------------+
                 |
                 |
+----------------------------------+
|     Desktop (Vision Node)        |
|                                  |
|   +--------------------------+   /
|   |       Vision Node        |  |
|   +------------+-------------+   /
|                |                 |
+----------------+-----------------+
```

1.2.2 The Case for Python in Robotics

While C++ is also a popular choice for robotics development—particularly for performance-critical components—**Python** has carved out a special niche:

- **Ease of Learning:** Python's syntax is simple and readable, making it approachable for beginners.

- **Rich Ecosystem:** Libraries such as **NumPy**, **SciPy**, **OpenCV**, and **TensorFlow** give you access to powerful tools for math, image processing, and machine learning.

- **Flexible Scripting:** Many robotic tasks involve rapid prototyping, and Python's interpretive nature allows you to quickly test ideas or fix bugs.

- **Strong ROS2 Support:** ROS2's Python client library, **rclpy**, provides a convenient **API** for creating nodes, publishers, subscribers, services, and actions without the overhead of C++.

Rhetorical Question: If you can write sophisticated algorithms to control a fleet of robots using a simple, readable language like Python, why not take advantage of that simplicity?

1.2.3 The Perfect Pair: Why ROS2 + Python is Ideal

1. **Rapid Prototyping**: Python's high-level abstractions let you spin up prototypes quickly.

2. **Broad Community**: There's a vast online community of ROS2 and Python developers, making it easier to find tutorials, sample code, and troubleshooting tips.

3. **Easy Integration**: You can tie in advanced data processing (e.g., neural networks) with ROS2 nodes via Python, bridging the gap between robotics and AI seamlessly.

4. **Beginner-Friendly**: For new roboticists, the combination drastically lowers initial barriers, allowing you to focus on **robot behaviors** rather than low-level infrastructure.

Analogy: Think of ROS2 as the "connective tissue" among all robot parts—sensors, motors, algorithms—and Python as a powerful "brain" that can interpret, decide, and instruct. Together, they create an agile, adaptable robotic system.

1.3 Setting Up Your Development Environment (ROS2, Python, and IDEs)

Now that you see the compelling reason to use ROS2 and Python, it's time to prepare your toolbox. Getting your environment set up is **critical** for a smooth robotics journey, as a misconfigured setup can lead to frustrating errors down the line.

1.3.1 Overview of the Process

We'll proceed in four main steps:

1. **Decide on Your Operating System** (Linux, Windows, or macOS).

2. **Install ROS2** for your chosen OS.

3. **Install Python** (if not already installed).

4. **Choose an Integrated Development Environment (IDE)** to streamline your coding and debugging workflows.

Diagram 2: *Typical ROS2 Development Setup*

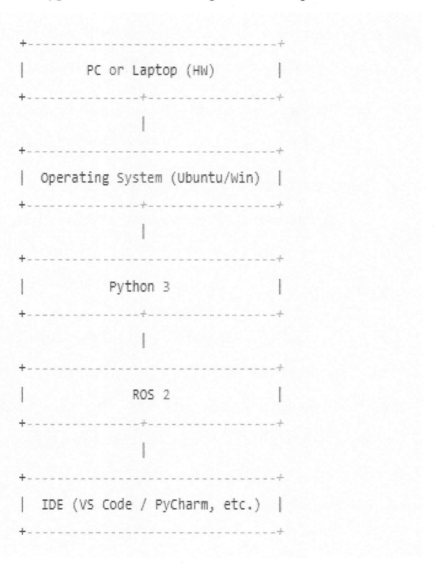

1.3.2 Choosing an Operating System

1.3.2.1 Linux (Ubuntu Recommended)

Most advanced ROS2 tutorials and guides assume **Ubuntu** because ROS2 was initially developed on Linux and remains best supported there. If you're comfortable with Linux—or willing to learn—it's often the **path of least resistance**.

- **Installation**: You can dual-boot Ubuntu alongside your existing OS or use a virtual machine like VirtualBox.

- **Support**: You'll find the largest set of official documentation and community Q&A for Ubuntu-based installations.

1.3.2.2 Windows

If you prefer staying on Windows, ROS2 has official support as well. The process typically involves installing Visual Studio build tools, CMake, and a few other dependencies. You may also run **ROS2** inside the Windows Subsystem for Linux (WSL), combining the convenience of Windows with a Linux-like environment.

1.3.2.3 macOS

ROS2 can be installed on macOS, although community support and available packages might be less extensive than Ubuntu. Still, if macOS is your daily driver, you can follow official instructions using the Homebrew package manager.

Tip: If you are brand-new to robotics and don't have a strong preference, Ubuntu might be your best bet. You'll find the most up-to-date documentation, forum answers, and tutorials.

1.3.3 Installing ROS2

Each ROS2 distribution (e.g., **Foxy**, **Galactic**, **Humble**) has slightly different requirements. Always consult the official ROS2 documentation for the specific version you plan to use.

1. **Add the ROS2 GPG Key and Repository:** This tells your system's package manager where to fetch ROS2 components from.

2. **Install the Desired ROS2 Packages:** For example, ros-foxy-desktop or ros-humble-desktop, which includes standard tools like RViz, demos, and navigation.

3. **Source Your ROS2 Environment:** Run something like:

bash

```
source /opt/ros/foxy/setup.bash
```
so your terminal knows about ROS2 commands. You might add this to your ~/.bashrc for convenience.

Note: *The exact commands depend on your chosen OS and ROS2 distribution. Following the official step-by-step guide ensures a smooth installation.*

1.3.4 Installing Python (If Needed)

Chances are, your operating system already includes Python 3. Check by opening a terminal (or command prompt) and typing:

css

```
python3 --version
```
If you need Python or a newer version:

- On **Ubuntu:**

sql

```
sudo apt update
```

```
sudo apt install python3 python3-pip
```

- On **Windows**:

    o Download the installer from Python.org.

    o Be sure to check "Add Python to PATH" during the installation.

- On **macOS**:

    o Use the official Python installer or Homebrew (brew install python3).

Possible Gotcha: Always confirm that when you type python3, it points to the right version. Mismatched or incomplete Python installations can cause cryptic errors later.

1.3.5 Picking an IDE

Integrated Development Environments (IDEs) can significantly streamline your workflow with features like syntax highlighting, code suggestions, integrated terminals, and built-in debugging.

Popular Choices

1. **Visual Studio Code (VS Code)**

- o Free, cross-platform, actively maintained.

- o Extensive extensions for Python, ROS2, Docker, and more.

- o Built-in Git integration for version control.

2. **PyCharm**

- o Excellent for Python projects, offers auto-completion, debugging, testing frameworks.

- o Community Edition is free; Professional adds advanced features like remote development.

3. **Eclipse or CLion**

- o More advanced users might prefer these for large projects or multi-language codebases.

- o Overkill for beginners but very powerful for integrated C++ and Python development.

Step-by-Step:

1. Download and install your IDE of choice.

2. Install relevant plugins (e.g., a ROS extension, Python extension).

[41]

3. Configure your IDE to source the ROS2 setup script automatically (often by editing a project-specific settings file).

1.3.6 Validating Your Setup

It's wise to do a quick "Hello World" test to ensure everything works together.

1. **Open a Terminal** and verify ROS2 installation:

```bash
```

```
ros2 --help
```
If you see a list of commands, ROS2 is recognized.

2. **Check Python:**

```css
```

```
python3 --version
```

3. **Run a ROS2 Demo** (optional):

```arduino
```

```
ros2 run demo_nodes_cpp talker
```
In another terminal, try:

```arduino
```

```
ros2 run demo_nodes_py listener
```

Confirm that messages pass between them—this ensures your networking and environment configuration are correct.

Diagram 3: *Environment Setup Flowchart*

```
+-------------------+
|   Choose OS      |
+-------------------+
         |
+---------------------+
|  Install ROS 2     |
+---------------------+
         |
+-----------------------------------+
|  Install/Check Python 3          |
+-----------------------------------+
            |
+-------------------------------+
|  Install an IDE              |
|  (VS Code/PyCharm)           |
+-------------------------------+
            |
+-------------------------------+
|  Verify Installation         |
+-------------------------------+
            |
+------------------+
|  Success        |
+------------------+
```

1.4 Key Concepts and Terminology

Robotics—and ROS2 in particular—introduces a unique vocabulary. Before you start programming robots, it helps to have a mental map of the core terms you'll encounter. Below is a quick glossary to prevent confusion later on.

1.4.1 Nodes

A **node** is a fundamental executable that performs a specific task within the ROS2 ecosystem. Instead of creating one massive program handling sensors, motors, and logic all in one place, ROS2 encourages you to split tasks into separate nodes. This modularity makes your system:

- **Easier to debug** (isolating issues in one node without impacting others).

- **More flexible** (you can replace or upgrade one node without rewriting the entire codebase).

- **Scalable** (nodes can be distributed across multiple machines on the same network).

Analogy: Think of each node like a different shop in a marketplace—one might sell produce, another might sell baked goods. They're all part of the same market (your robot), but each does its own job.

1.4.2 Topics

A **topic** is a named channel through which nodes exchange messages in a **publish-subscribe** manner. One node **publishes** data (like camera images, sensor readings, or velocity commands) to a topic, and other nodes **subscribe** to receive that data in real time.

- **One-Way Communication**: There's no built-in feedback mechanism—publishers don't know which subscribers, if any, are listening.

- **Data Streams**: Best used for continuous streams of data, such as sensor feeds or ongoing status updates.

1.4.3 Messages

A **message** is the data structure being transmitted across a topic. ROS2 predefines many standard message types (e.g., std_msgs/msg/String or sensor_msgs/msg/Image). You can also create **custom message types** to suit your specific needs (like a GPS coordinate message with latitude, longitude, and altitude).

Clarity: These messages define the shape and type of data— just as a letter in the mail has an envelope specifying what's inside.

1.4.4 Services

While topics are perfect for streaming data, sometimes you need a **request-response** pattern. For instance, if you want to trigger a specific action, like "Start the conveyor belt," and then wait for a response ("Conveyor belt started"), you'd use a **service**. One node **offers** the service, and another **calls** it:

- **Synchronous Interaction**: The client waits for the server to respond.

- **Discrete Events**: Services are typically used for tasks that begin and end with a clear request and reply.

1.4.5 Actions

If you have a **long-running** process—for instance, instructing a robot to navigate across a warehouse floor while sending progress updates—**actions** are ideal. They extend services by providing **feedback** (e.g., "I'm 50% along the route") and a **result** once the action completes. This structure is more complex but invaluable for tasks that don't finish instantly.

1.4.6 Parameter Server

ROS2 allows nodes to load **parameters**—like speed limits, sensor calibration values, or operational modes—from external configuration files. This means you can tweak certain values **without modifying code**. By referencing parameters at runtime, you can quickly test different settings.

Example: In a line-follower robot, the threshold for detecting a black line on a white floor could be stored in a parameter. By adjusting that threshold in a YAML file, you can fine-tune performance without delving into the source code.

1.4.7 Workspaces and Packages

ROS2 code is organized into **packages**, which are directories containing your scripts, message definitions, configuration files, and more. Multiple packages often reside in a single **workspace** (a folder you build and source), allowing for a clean, modular approach.

- **Workspace:** The root-level directory, often named something like ros2_ws. It contains src/ (source code) and other folders that appear once you build (like build/ or install/).

- **Package**: Each package has its own package.xml (ROS2 metadata) and either a setup.py (for Python) or a CMakeLists.txt (for C++).

Rhetorical Question: Isn't it easier to keep your code neat and collaborative when everything is logically partitioned? Absolutely!

1.4.8 Simulation and Visualization Tools

While not strictly part of the "core" terminology, **simulation** (e.g., using Gazebo or Ignition) and **visualization** (e.g., using RViz) are central to many ROS2 workflows:

- **Simulation**: Let's you test your robot software in a virtual environment with gravity, friction, and realistic sensor models.

- **Visualization**: Tools like RViz show sensor data, robot models, and navigation maps in real time, helping you debug and fine-tune algorithms.

1.4.9 Putting It All Together

Once you grasp nodes, topics, services, actions, messages, parameters, packages, and workspaces, you've got a bird's-eye view of how ROS2 systems are structured. You'll use these concepts over and over—**from controlling a single motor** to **managing an entire swarm** of autonomous drones.

Chapter Summary

You've just completed an in-depth introduction to **getting started with ROS2 and Python**. This first chapter aimed to give you a clear, jargon-free understanding of why robotics is so powerful and how ROS2 plus Python provide a robust framework for designing, testing, and deploying robot applications.

Key Takeaways:

1. **Robotics Foundations**: Robots sense, think, and act. Their potential spans manufacturing, healthcare, exploration, and beyond.

2. **Why ROS2 Matters**: ROS2's modular architecture and real-time, cross-platform capabilities address the challenges faced by modern, complex robotics systems.

3. **The Python Advantage**: Python's ease of use and vast ecosystem make it an excellent language for rapid

prototyping, data processing, and integration with ROS2.

4. **Environment Setup:** Decide on an OS (often Ubuntu for best support), install ROS2, set up Python, and select an IDE. Verify your environment with quick demos to ensure everything is working.

5. **Core Terminology:** Nodes, topics, services, actions, messages, parameters, packages, and workspaces are the fundamental building blocks in ROS2.

__Final Rhetorical Question__: Are you ready to transform ideas into action by harnessing the synergy of ROS2 and Python? The journey may seem long, but the foundations you've built here will make the path more approachable and the results more rewarding.

What's Next?

In subsequent chapters, you'll:

- **Dive deeper** into ROS2's core concepts—like advanced communication, debugging, and system structuring.

- **Explore Python fundamentals** specifically tailored for robotics, such as using **NumPy** and **OpenCV** for sensor data processing.

- **Build hands-on projects** that gradually escalate in complexity, ensuring you learn by doing, not just by reading.

Keep this chapter as your quick reference guide to **why** and **how** we use ROS2 and Python in robotics. The next steps will show you **exactly what** to do with these tools to bring your robotic dreams to life.

Chapter 2: Core Concepts of ROS2

In the realm of modern robotics, having a robust framework that eases inter-process communication, hardware abstraction, and code organization is not just a luxury—it's a necessity. **ROS2** (Robot Operating System 2) addresses these needs by providing a unified platform where developers can create, run, and scale robotic applications with minimal friction. Whether you're building a small hobby project or a large industrial solution, ROS2's modular design shines by simplifying how robots **perceive, plan, and act** in their environments.

This chapter serves as your comprehensive guide to ROS2's central concepts. You'll learn how ROS2 breaks down a robot's software into **nodes,** how those nodes exchange information via **topics, services,** and **actions,** and how you can organize your code into **packages** and **workspaces.** We'll dive deep into ROS2's **communication mechanisms,** exploring how it seamlessly handles the discovery of nodes and the transport of messages. We'll also look at **launch files** for orchestrating complex systems and **parameter servers** for easily tuning your robot's behavior. Finally, we'll cap things off with a **hands-on section** where you build and run your very first ROS2 node in Python. By the end of this chapter, you should have the conceptual and practical skills to begin assembling fully functional robot software.

Let's dive in!

2.1 Nodes, Topics, Services, and Actions

One of the first things you'll notice about a ROS2-based system is how the functionality is broken into discrete components. Instead of writing a single, colossal program that does everything—sensor reading, motor control, path planning—ROS2 encourages you to write multiple **nodes** that each have a single responsibility. To facilitate communication among these nodes, ROS2 offers a **publish-subscribe** model (topics) and a **request-response** model (services and actions). Let's unpack each of these core building blocks one by one.

2.1.1 Nodes: The Fundamental Units of Computation

A **node** in ROS2 is an executable that contains all the logic required for a specific task or set of closely related tasks. For instance, you might have one node responsible for reading temperature data from a sensor, another for controlling a servo motor, and yet another for handling object detection. By decentralizing your application into nodes, you:

1. **Improve Maintainability:** If something breaks, you only need to troubleshoot or replace the defective node.

2. **Encourage Code Reuse:** Nodes that solve a particular problem (e.g., a node that calculates odometry) can be reused across multiple projects.

3. **Enhance Clarity:** Each node's functionality is self-contained, making it easy for new team members to understand and contribute.

Rhetorical Question: Would you prefer one giant file with 10,000 lines of code, or a set of smaller, clearly labeled "mini programs" that each handle a well-defined task? ROS2's node-centric architecture embraces the latter approach for good reason.

2.1.2 Topics: Sharing Data in Real Time (Publish-Subscribe)

If nodes are the building blocks, **topics** are the roads that connect them. A **topic** is a named communication channel where one or more nodes can **publish** or **subscribe** to data streams.

- **Publisher:** A node that emits (sends out) data to a topic.

- **Subscriber:** A node that listens (receives data) from that topic.

For example, a laser scanner node might publish a stream of distance measurements to a topic called /scan. Simultaneously, a mapping node subscribes to /scan, using the data to build or update a map of the environment.

Key Traits of Topics

1. **Unidirectional**: Data flows one way—from publishers to subscribers—there's no built-in feedback mechanism.

2. **Many-to-Many**: Multiple nodes can publish to the same topic, and multiple nodes can subscribe to it, creating flexible data pipelines.

Analogy: Think of a radio station (the publisher) broadcasting music on a certain frequency (the topic). Anyone with a radio receiver tuned to that frequency (the subscriber) can listen. However, the radio station doesn't inherently know who's listening or how many people are tuned in.

2.1.3 Services: Synchronous Request-Response

Occasionally, you'll need more structured interaction: one node asks another node to do something and waits for a **yes/no** or a result. **Services** enable this request-response pattern. Typically, you'll see them used for tasks that aren't continuous data streams but short, discrete commands, such as:

- Turning on a specific sensor.
- Checking if a component is calibrated.
- Sending a single command to open a robotic gripper.

When a node needs something done, it calls a service with a request message. The node that **offers** the service processes the request and sends back a response message.

Why Services Over Topics?

1. **Immediate Feedback**: The calling node knows if the request succeeded or failed.

2. **Stateful Interaction**: Services can handle tasks that need a decision or user interaction, like "start conveyor belt" or "stop conveyor belt."

2.1.4 Actions: Handling Long-Running Tasks with Feedback

While services are ideal for quick, synchronous tasks, some operations take longer and benefit from intermediate updates. **Actions** are designed for these scenarios. Think of commanding a mobile robot to move from one side of a warehouse to the other. That's not an instantaneous job—there could be obstacles, changing conditions, or partial progress updates.

Actions provide:

- **Goal**: The request to do something (like "navigate to x=10, y=5").

- **Feedback**: Periodic updates while the action is running (e.g., "25% of the path covered").

- **Result**: A final report when the task completes or fails.

Rhetorical Question: Imagine you send a robot off to deliver a package—would you prefer to have absolutely no idea how it's doing, or receive timely progress reports? That's the difference between a simple service call and an action with feedback.

2.1.5 Diagram 1: Node Interactions Overview

```
+-------------------------------------+
|            Camera Node          |
|---------------------------------/
| Publishes Topic:                |
|    /camera_images               |
+----------------+----------------+
                 |
                 v
+-------------------------------------+
| Object Detection Node|
|---------------------------------/
| Subscribes to:                  |
|    /camera_images               |
| Offers Service:                 |
|    /detect_objects              |
+----------------+----------------+
                 |
(Service Call: /detect_objects)
                 |
                 v
+-------------------------------------+
| Motion Control Node   |
|---------------------------------/
| Calls Service:                  |
|    /detect_objects              |
| Uses Action Server:             |
|    /navigate_to_pose            |
+-------------------------------------+
```

2.2 Packages and Workspaces: Organizing Your Project

Once you're comfortable with the "nodes talk via topics/services/actions" model, the next big question is: **how do I organize all my code and resources**? ROS2 addresses this with **packages** and **workspaces**, offering a clean, modular structure that fosters collaboration and maintainability.

2.2.1 ROS2 Packages: Bundling Functionality

A **ROS2 package** is essentially a folder containing all the files needed to perform one or more related tasks. This could include:

- **Source code** (Python scripts or C++ files).

- **Message definitions** (for custom message types).

- **Launch files** (we'll get to these shortly).

- **Configuration** (e.g., YAML or URDF files describing robots and sensors).

- **Package metadata** (like package.xml or setup.py).

By grouping logically related files (for example, everything related to controlling a particular sensor or a specific algorithm) into a single package, you can:

1. **Reuse** that package across multiple projects.

2. **Share** it easily with the ROS2 community.

3. **Test** and **maintain** it as an isolated component.

Analogy: If your entire robot project was a book, each package would be a chapter focusing on one key topic or function, complete with its own references and diagrams.

2.2.2 Workspaces: Your Project's Ecosystem

A **workspace** is a top-level directory where one or more ROS2 packages reside. It usually contains subfolders like src/ (for source code), build/, install/, and log/ after you've compiled. By default, many developers name their workspace something like ros2_ws or my_robot_ws.

1. **src/ Folder**: Houses all your ROS2 packages.

2. **build/ Folder**: Created automatically when you run the build system (colcon build), holding intermediate build files.

3. **install/ Folder**: Contains final, compiled binaries and scripts, making your packages ready to run.

4. **log/ Folder**: Stores logs from your running or tested nodes, which is crucial for debugging.

Best Practice: Keep each workspace focused on a particular robot or project scope, especially if you're dealing with numerous packages or different hardware configurations.

2.2.3 Diagram 2: Typical ROS2 Workspace Structure

```
my_robot_ws/
├── src/
│   ├── my_sensors_package/
│   │   ├── package.xml
│   │   ├── setup.py
│   │   ├── launch/
│   │   │   └── my_sensors_launch.py
│   │   └── ...
│   └── my_navigation_package/
│       ├── package.xml
│       ├── setup.py
│       ├── launch/
│       │   └── my_navigation_launch.py
│       └── ...
├── build/
│   └── (build artifacts after colcon build)
├── install/
│   └── (installed executables, libraries, etc.)
└── log/
    └── (log files from node output and other tools)
```

2.2.4 Creating a Package: Step-by-Step

1. **Navigate to Your Workspace**

```bash
cd ~/my_robot_ws/src
```

2. **Use the ROS2 CLI**

```lua
ros2 pkg create --build-type ament_python my_example_package
```

- o my_example_package is your new package's name.

- o --build-type ament_python indicates it's a Python-based package (for C++, use ament_cmake).

3. **Modify Package Files**

- o package.xml holds meta-information (e.g., name, version, description).

- o setup.py configures how Python code is installed and run.

4. **Add Source Code**

- o Create a my_example_package/my_example_package/ folder for Python scripts.

- o Write your node logic in .py files inside that folder.

5. **Build and Source**

bash

```
cd ~/my_robot_ws
colcon build
source install/setup.bash
```

Reminder: *Always remember to* **source** *your newly built workspace so that ROS2 knows about your packages.*

2.3 ROS2 Communication Mechanisms

How does ROS2 ensure that nodes automatically find each other on a network and exchange data smoothly? Under the hood, ROS2 relies on something called **DDS (Data Distribution Service)**. It manages **discovery, message transport**, and **Quality of Service (QoS)**. This section dives deeper into those details, clarifying why ROS2 is so effective for distributed robotics applications.

2.3.1 DDS and Discovery

DDS is a middleware protocol specifically designed for real-time, distributed systems. In ROS2, each node broadcasts information about who it is and what topics/services/actions it provides or uses. Other nodes that share the same **ROS2**

domain automatically discover these broadcasts, forming a peer-to-peer network.

Rhetorical Question: How convenient is it that you don't have to manually configure IP addresses or port numbers for each node? DDS does that heavy lifting, letting you focus on the actual robot logic.

2.3.2 Quality of Service (QoS) Settings

Robotic data streams are not all created equal. For some topics (e.g., teleoperation commands), you might need **reliable** message delivery at all costs. For others (e.g., a high-frame-rate camera feed), losing a few frames might be acceptable if it reduces lag. **QoS profiles** let you fine-tune how data is transported:

- **Reliability**: Choose between "reliable" (guaranteed delivery) or "best-effort" (faster, but messages can get dropped).

- **Durability**: Keep messages for late-joining subscribers, or only transmit the newest data.

- **Deadline**: Set time limits by which data must be delivered.

Example: A node controlling an industrial arm might need guaranteed, reliable commands. A node streaming video to a user interface can tolerate occasional drops to maintain real-time performance.

2.3.3 Diagram 3: ROS2 Communication Under the Hood

```
+----------------------------------------------+
|         Node A (Publishes Topic X)           |
|----------------------------------------------/
|   e.g., camera_node, sensor_node, etc.       |
+----------------------------------------------+
                   ^ (calls into)
+----------------------------------------------+
|   ROS2 Client Libraries (rclcpp/rclpy)       |
|----------------------------------------------/
|   Offers high-level APIs for Topics,         |
|   Services, Actions, etc.                    |
+----------------------------------------------+
                   ^ (uses DDS)
+----------------------------------------------+
|   DDS: Discovery, QoS, Transport             |
|----------------------------------------------/
|   Handles peer-to-peer communication         |
|   across networks (wired, WiFi, etc.)        |
+----------------------------------------------+
| Network (Physical or Virtual)                |
+----------------------------------------------+
                   ^ (DDS messages flow)
+----------------------------------------------+
|         Node B (Subscribes Topic X)          |
|----------------------------------------------/
| e.g., object_detection_node, etc.            |
+----------------------------------------------+
```

2.3.4 Multi-Machine Systems

One of ROS2's greatest strengths is how straightforward it is to run nodes on multiple machines, provided they're connected via a network:

1. **Same Domain**: By default, nodes share a domain ID. If two machines have the same domain ID and can communicate via network, their nodes discover each other automatically.

2. **Zero Manual Configuration**: Thanks to DDS, you don't typically have to specify IP addresses or ports.

3. **Load Distribution**: This makes it simple to offload heavy computations (like machine learning inference) to more powerful computers, while real-time tasks run on a smaller embedded board.

2.4 Launch Files and Parameter Servers

As your robot application grows in complexity, manually starting each node with specific configurations becomes cumbersome. That's where **launch files** and the **parameter server** concept come into play, making it easy to orchestrate your entire robot software stack and tweak behaviors on the fly.

2.4.1 Launch Files: Automating Node Startup

A **launch file**—written in Python for ROS2—lets you define which nodes should run, what parameters to load, and how outputs should be handled. Instead of opening multiple terminals and typing commands manually, you can start everything with:

```
ros2 launch my_example_package my_robot_launch.py
```

Key Elements of Launch Files

1. **Node Definitions**: Specify the package name, executable name, and optional parameters.

2. **Remappings**: Change the name of a topic or service at runtime if needed.

3. **Grouping and Conditional Launch**: Launch certain nodes only if specific conditions are met (e.g., simulation vs. real hardware).

Benefit: If your robot has 10 different nodes, one well-written launch file can spin them all up with a single command—no more copy-pasting multiple terminal commands or forgetting a crucial node.

2.4.2 Parameter Servers: Flexible Configuration

Parameters let you alter how nodes behave without changing your source code. Typically, these are numeric or string values stored in a YAML file. For example:

```yaml

my_robot_controller:
  ros__parameters:
    max_speed: 1.0
    turn_rate: 0.5
```

When your node starts, it reads these parameter values and configures its internal logic accordingly. You might have:

- **max_speed** controlling the maximum linear velocity of a mobile robot.

- **turn_rate** specifying how sharply it can pivot.

Adjusting parameters is as simple as editing the YAML and relaunching (or dynamically updating, if your node supports it). This approach saves significant time since you don't have to recompile each time you want to test new settings.

Why Bother with Parameters?

1. **Tuning**: Fine-tune your robot's performance in real-world environments.

2. **Reusability:** The same code can run multiple robots with different characteristics—just change the parameter files.

3. **Deployment:** Shift from a testing environment to production by loading different parameter sets for each scenario.

2.5 Hands-On: Building Your First ROS2 Node in Python

It's time to roll up your sleeves and get practical. In this section, you'll **create a basic ROS2 package** containing **two Python nodes:** one that **publishes** random data (simulating a sensor), and one that **subscribes** to that data (simulating a processor). By the end of this exercise, you'll have experienced the entire workflow—from package creation to node execution.

2.5.1 Prerequisites

- A functioning **ROS2** installation.

- **Python 3** installed and recognized by your system.

- A **workspace** already created (e.g., ~/my_robot_ws) and sourced.

2.5.2 Step 1: Create a Package

1. **Navigate to Your Workspace's src Folder**

```bash
bash
```

```bash
cd ~/my_robot_ws/src
```

2. **Run the Package Creation Command**

```lua
lua
```

```
ros2 pkg create --build-type ament_python
sensor_demo
```

3. **Check the Generated Files**

```bash
bash
```

```bash
cd sensor_demo
tree
```

You'll see a structure that includes package.xml, setup.py, and a folder named sensor_demo/ for your Python scripts.

2.5.3 Step 2: Write the Publisher Node

Inside sensor_demo/sensor_demo/, create a file named random_sensor.py:

```python
python
```

```python
#!/usr/bin/env python3

import rclpy
from rclpy.node import Node
from std_msgs.msg import Float32
import random
```

```python
class RandomSensor(Node):
    def __init__(self):
        super().__init__('random_sensor_node')
        # Publisher that publishes Float32
messages to the 'sensor_data' topic
        self.publisher_ =
self.create_publisher(Float32, 'sensor_data', 10)
        # Timer calls publish_data() every second
        self.timer_ = self.create_timer(1.0,
self.publish_data)

    def publish_data(self):
        msg = Float32()
        # Generate a random value between 0 and
100
        msg.data = random.uniform(0, 100)
        self.get_logger().info(f'Publishing
Sensor Data: {msg.data:.2f}')
        self.publisher_.publish(msg)

def main(args=None):
    rclpy.init(args=args)
    node = RandomSensor()
    rclpy.spin(node)
    node.destroy_node()
    rclpy.shutdown()
```

```
if __name__ == '__main__':
    main()
```

Breakdown

- **Node Initialization:** The class RandomSensor inherits from Node, giving it ROS2 capabilities.

- **Publisher Creation:** create_publisher() sets up a topic named sensor_data where messages of type Float32 are sent.

- **Timer:** The create_timer() method calls publish_data() every second (1.0 second interval).

- **publish_data():** Generates a random float, logs it, and publishes it as a Float32 message.

2.5.4 Step 3: Write the Subscriber Node

Still inside sensor_demo/sensor_demo/, create another file named data_listener.py:

python

```
#!/usr/bin/env python3

import rclpy
from rclpy.node import Node
from std_msgs.msg import Float32

class DataListener(Node):
    def __init__(self):
```

```python
        super().__init__('data_listener_node')
        self.subscription_ =
self.create_subscription(
            Float32,
            'sensor_data',
            self.data_callback,
            10
        )

    def data_callback(self, msg):
        self.get_logger().info(f'Received Data:
{msg.data:.2f}')

def main(args=None):
    rclpy.init(args=args)
    node = DataListener()
    rclpy.spin(node)
    node.destroy_node()
    rclpy.shutdown()

if __name__ == '__main__':
    main()
```

Breakdown

- **Subscriber:** The create_subscription() method instructs ROS2 to listen for Float32 messages on the sensor_data topic.

- **Callback**: Whenever a new message arrives, data_callback() is executed, logging the received value.

2.5.5 Step 4: Update setup.py

In sensor_demo/setup.py, ensure you have the following entry_points so **ROS2** can recognize your executables:

```python
from setuptools import setup

package_name = 'sensor_demo'

setup(
    name=package_name,
    version='0.0.1',
    packages=[package_name],
    data_files=[

('share/ament_index/resource_index/packages',
            ['resource/' + package_name]),
        ('share/' + package_name,
['package.xml']),
    ],
    install_requires=['setuptools'],
    zip_safe=True,
    maintainer='YourName',
    maintainer_email='YourEmail@example.com',
```

```
    description='Demo package for learning ROS2
publishing and subscribing',
    license='Apache License 2.0',
    tests_require=['pytest'],
    entry_points={
        'console_scripts': [
            'random_sensor =
sensor_demo.random_sensor:main',
            'data_listener =
sensor_demo.data_listener:main',
        ],
    },
)
```

2.5.6 Step 5: Make Scripts Executable

bash

```
cd sensor_demo/sensor_demo
chmod +x random_sensor.py
chmod +x data_listener.py
```

2.5.7 Step 6: Build and Source

1. Return to Your Workspace Root

bash

```
cd ~/my_robot_ws
```

2. **Build**

```
colcon build
```

3. **Source**

```bash
bash
```

```
source install/setup.bash
```

4. **Verify**

```perl
perl
```

```
ros2 pkg list | grep sensor_demo
```

You should see sensor_demo in the output.

2.5.8 Step 7: Run the Nodes

Open two terminals (or use two tabs in one terminal window). In the first:

```arduino
arduino
```

```
ros2 run sensor_demo random_sensor
```

In the second:

```arduino
arduino
```

```
ros2 run sensor_demo data_listener
```

Observing the Output

- **Publisher Terminal**: Logs "Publishing Sensor Data: XX.xx" every second.

- **Subscriber Terminal**: Logs "Received Data: XX.xx" matching the published values.

Congratulations—you've built, launched, and verified a **working ROS2 system** with nodes that publish and subscribe to a shared topic. This fundamental pattern—**publishing from one node, subscribing from another**—repeats across countless robotics scenarios, from reading temperature sensors to streaming HD camera feeds.

2.5.9 Creating a Simple Launch File (Optional)

To simplify running both nodes, create a launch file in sensor_demo/launch/sensor_demo_launch.py:

```java
from launch import LaunchDescription
from launch_ros.actions import Node

def generate_launch_description():
    return LaunchDescription([
        Node(
            package='sensor_demo',
            executable='random_sensor',
            name='random_sensor_node'
        ),
        Node(
            package='sensor_demo',
```

```
        executable='data_listener',
        name='data_listener_node'
    ),
])
```

Then:

```
ros2 launch sensor_demo sensor_demo_launch.py
```

Both nodes will start automatically, saving you from manual terminal commands.

Chapter Summary

You've just acquired a **solid foundation** in ROS2, delving deep into its **core concepts**: nodes, topics, services, actions, workspaces, packages, communication mechanics, launch files, and parameter configuration. Let's recap what we covered and **why it matters**:

1. **Nodes, Topics, Services, and Actions:**

   o **Nodes** break your robot logic into manageable chunks.

   o **Topics** provide streaming, publish-subscribe data channels.

   o **Services** enable request-response for short, discrete tasks.

   o **Actions** handle long-running tasks that provide intermediate feedback.

2. **Packages and Workspaces**:

  - **Packages** group related files—scripts, configuration, and dependencies—into tidy modules.

  - **Workspaces** hold multiple packages, forming an ecosystem for your entire robotics project.

3. **ROS2 Communication Mechanisms**:

  - **DDS** underlies how nodes discover each other without manual **IP** configuration.

  - **QoS** (Quality of Service) lets you tailor reliability, latency, and resource usage for each data channel.

4. **Launch Files and Parameter Servers**:

  - **Launch files** coordinate multiple nodes, letting you spin up entire robot systems with a single command.

  - **Parameter servers** (or parameter configuration) allow dynamic tuning of robot behaviors without touching your source code.

5. **Hands-On Project**:

  - You built your first two ROS2 Python nodes— one publishing random data, one subscribing and logging it.

o You optionally explored a **launch file** to streamline node management.

*No Repetition: Each concept introduced here enriches your ROS2 knowledge without duplicating earlier content about installing or setting up the environment. That means you've taken a **significant leap** in your robotics skill set—traversing from abstract understanding to **practical implementation**.*

Looking Ahead

What can you do with this knowledge?

- **Expand** your nodes to handle real sensor data. Instead of publishing random numbers, connect to an actual sensor (like a temperature sensor or IMU).

- **Integrate** advanced logic. For instance, add a service that calibrates your sensor or an action that instructs a robot arm to pick up an object.

- **Optimize** your code with QoS settings. Fine-tune reliability and throughput for specific use-cases.

- **Develop** parameterized nodes that read from a YAML file to handle sensor thresholds, control gains, or environment specifics.

- **Collaborate** with others by packaging your nodes into shareable ROS2 packages, ensuring consistent builds and versioning across the team.

As you advance, you'll find these core concepts repeated everywhere in the ROS2 ecosystem—from controlling swarm drones to building advanced industrial automation solutions. Understanding nodes, topics, services, actions, packages, and communication mechanisms is the bedrock upon which all your future robotics software rests.

Final Rhetorical Question: *Are you beginning to see how quickly you can scale up from this simple example to a fully functioning robot? With ROS2, the journey from first node to advanced application might be shorter than you think— especially now that you hold these foundational pieces.*

Chapter 3: Python Fundamentals for Robotics

Robotics is a field where **software** meets **hardware,** bridging the gap between code and the physical world. At the heart of this bridging process, **Python** stands out as a powerhouse language, recognized for its simplicity, readability, and extensive library ecosystem. From controlling motors and reading sensor data to applying sophisticated computer vision or machine learning algorithms, Python proves itself invaluable at every stage. This chapter offers a thorough exploration of **Python basics** (for readers who need a refresher), dives into the **key libraries** commonly used in robotics, and provides practical guidance on **writing efficient code, debugging, testing,** and even a hands-on project for **sensor data processing.**

By the end of this chapter, you'll have a strong grasp of how Python underpins many modern robotics workflows—and the confidence to start creating your own robotic solutions with minimal friction.

3.1 Python Basics Refresher (for Beginners)

3.1.1 Why Python in Robotics?

Before we dive into the technical nuts and bolts, let's briefly address **why Python is such a go-to language** in robotics. We've touched on this in previous contexts, but to reiterate in a purely Python-centric way:

- **Easy to Learn**: Python has a clear, intuitive syntax, reducing the overhead for new developers or roboticists transitioning from other fields.

- **Rich Ecosystem**: Whether you need to process images (OpenCV), handle large datasets (NumPy, Pandas), or implement neural networks (TensorFlow, PyTorch), Python's library support is unparalleled.

- **Rapid Prototyping**: In robotics, ideas evolve fast— Python lets you experiment without the compilation overhead of lower-level languages like C++.

- **Community Support**: With countless online resources, forums, and tutorials, it's easy to solve coding problems or find best practices.

Rhetorical Question: Isn't it more exciting to focus on the actual robot behavior rather than wrestle with a complex programming language? Python's simplicity allows you to do exactly that.

3.1.2 Core Python Syntax and Structures

If you're entirely new to Python or just need a quick refresher, let's walk through the fundamentals. **No complicated jargon**, just straightforward explanations.

Variables and Data Types

In Python, you don't need to declare variable types explicitly. You simply assign values, and Python infers the type:

```python
```

```python
distance = 10           # An integer
speed = 3.14            # A float (decimal)
robot_name = "Rover"    # A string
is_active = True        # A boolean (True/False)
```

Clarity: Python is dynamically typed, so distance can later hold a string or any other data type. However, that flexibility comes with responsibility: keep track of your variable usage to avoid confusion.

Basic Operators

- **Arithmetic Operators**: +, -, *, /, // (integer division), ** (exponent), % (modulus).

- **Comparison Operators**: ==, !=, <, >, <=, >=.

- **Logical Operators**: and, or, not.

```python
Example:
```

```python
```

```
distance_traveled = speed * time
if distance_traveled > 100:
    print("The robot traveled over 100 units!")
```

Collections (Lists, Tuples, Dictionaries)

Robotics data often involves arrays (e.g., sensor readings) or dictionaries (e.g., parameter sets). In Python:

- **Lists:** Mutable sequences, great for changing data. Example:

python

```
sensor_readings = [0.5, 1.2, 0.9]
sensor_readings.append(1.1)
```

- **Tuples:** Immutable sequences, used when data must remain constant. Example:

python

```
coordinates = (10, 20, 30)
```

- **Dictionaries:** Key-value pairs, perfect for storing settings or mapping. Example:

python

```
config = {"max_speed": 2.5, "min_speed": 0.2}
print(config["max_speed"])   # Output: 2.5
```

Control Flow (if, for, while)

Control flow statements let you **direct** your program's execution:

- **if** statements handle conditional logic:

python

```
if battery_level < 20:
    print("Battery is low, returning to charging
station.")
elif battery_level < 50:
    print("Battery is moderate.")
else:
    print("Battery is fine.")
```

for *loops iterate over sequences:*

python

```
for reading in sensor_readings:
    print(reading)
```

- **while** loops continue until a condition breaks:

python

```
while distance_traveled < 100:
    distance_traveled += speed
```

Analogy: *Think of an if statement like a fork in the road—if conditions are met, you go one way; otherwise, you take another path.*

Functions and Classes

In robotics, functions break down tasks (like data processing or motor control) into reusable pieces. Classes group related functions and data under one logical entity:

python

```
def calculate_distance(speed, time):
    return speed * time


class Robot:
    def __init__(self, name):
        self.name = name
        self.distance_traveled = 0

    def move(self, speed, time):
        self.distance_traveled +=
calculate_distance(speed, time)
        return self.distance_traveled
```

Reminder: *Classes are especially useful in robotics when modeling entities like sensors or motor controllers, each with their own properties and methods.*

3.1.3 Diagram 1: Python's Basic Building Blocks

```
+--------------------------------------------------+
|                    Variables                     |
|--------------------------------------------------|
| Store data in named references for reuse.        |
+--------------------------------------------------+
                        |
                        v
+--------------------------------------------------+
|                    Data Types                    |
|--------------------------------------------------|
| e.g., int, float, str, list, dict, etc.          |
| Define the nature and behavior of the stored data|
+--------------------------------------------------+
                        |
                        v
+--------------------------------------------------+
|                    Operators                     |
|--------------------------------------------------|
| Perform operations on variables & data types:    |
| e.g., +, -, *, /, //, ==, !=, in, etc.           |
+--------------------------------------------------+
                        |
                        v
+--------------------------------------------------+
|                   Control Flow                   |
|--------------------------------------------------|
| Direct the program's execution path:             |
| if, elif, else, for, while, break, continue, etc.|
+--------------------------------------------------+
                        |
                        v
+--------------------------------------------------+
|                    Functions                     |
|--------------------------------------------------|
| Group reusable logic into callable blocks:       |
| def my_function(...):                            |
+--------------------------------------------------+
                        |
                        v
+--------------------------------------------------+
|                     Classes                      |
|--------------------------------------------------|
| Define object-oriented structures and behaviors: |
| class MyClass: ...                               |
+--------------------------------------------------+
```

3.2 Essential Python Libraries for Robotics (NumPy, OpenCV, etc.)

While Python's standard library is powerful on its own, robotics typically demands specialized functionality—handling large matrices of sensor data, analyzing images for computer vision tasks, or managing concurrency for real-time operations. This section dives into some of the **most essential libraries** you'll likely use.

3.2.1 NumPy: Numerical Computing at Scale

NumPy is the bedrock of scientific computing in Python. It provides a **fast, flexible array object** called the ndarray and a suite of tools for manipulating these arrays.

Why NumPy Matters

1. **Array Operations**: Perform calculations on entire arrays without writing explicit loops.

2. **Vectorized Computations**: Speed up math tasks by leveraging optimized C/Fortran code under the hood.

3. **Foundational**: Libraries like OpenCV and TensorFlow also rely on NumPy arrays.

Example: If you have a LiDAR scan represented as a list of distances, you can transform it into a NumPy array for quick average, standard deviation, or filtering.

python

```
import numpy as np

distances = [1.2, 1.1, 0.9, 1.5, 1.3]
arr = np.array(distances)
print("Mean distance:", arr.mean())
```

3.2.2 OpenCV: Powerhouse for Computer Vision

OpenCV (Open Source Computer Vision Library) is a robust toolkit for **image processing** and **computer vision**. Common robotics use-cases include:

- **Object Detection**: Identifying shapes, colors, or patterns.

- **Feature Extraction**: Finding corners, edges, or key points in an image.

- **Image Transformations**: Scaling, rotating, cropping images for downstream analysis.

Example: Converting an image to grayscale and blurring it to reduce noise:

```python
import cv2

image = cv2.imread("example.jpg")  # BGR format
gray = cv2.cvtColor(image, cv2.COLOR_BGR2GRAY)
blurred = cv2.GaussianBlur(gray, (5, 5), 0)
```

```
cv2.imshow("Blurred Image", blurred)
cv2.waitKey(0)
```

Rhetorical Question: *Could your robot autonomously navigate a cluttered room without advanced vision techniques? It's tricky, which is why OpenCV is so pivotal.*

3.2.3 Matplotlib & Plotly: Visualizing Data

For debugging or understanding sensor data, **visualization** is invaluable. **Matplotlib** is the classic Python plotting library; **Plotly** offers interactive charts. You might:

- Plot sensor readings over time to observe anomalies.
- Visualize real-time data from a camera or LiDAR scan.
- Create histograms to see distribution of measured distances.

Matplotlib Example:

```python
import matplotlib.pyplot as plt

time = [0, 1, 2, 3, 4]
values = [10, 12, 15, 20, 25]
plt.plot(time, values)
plt.title("Distance Over Time")
plt.xlabel("Time (s)")
plt.ylabel("Distance (m)")
```

```
plt.show()
```

3.2.4 SciPy & scikit-learn: Advanced Processing and ML

SciPy extends NumPy with modules for **optimization, signal processing**, and more. **scikit-learn** is a user-friendly library for **machine learning** tasks like classification, regression, and clustering. In robotics, you might:

- Use SciPy's **signal filters** to smooth sensor data.

- Train a scikit-learn **classifier** to detect objects or anomalies in sensor readings.

3.2.5 Additional Tools and Libraries

- **Pandas**: Handy for tabular data, though less common for real-time robotics.

- **PyTorch / TensorFlow**: For neural networks in advanced perception or planning tasks.

- **pyserial**: For **serial communication** with microcontrollers or sensors.

- **asyncio**: To handle **asynchronous** operations, crucial for real-time or event-driven robotics.

3.2.6 Diagram 2: The Python Robotics Ecosystem

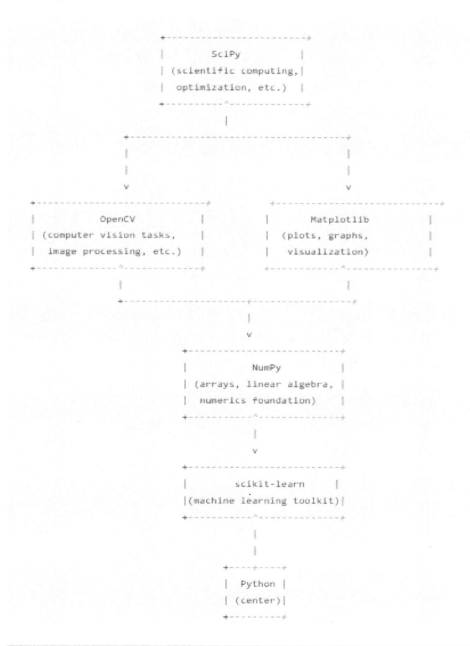

3.3 Writing Efficient and Clean Python Code

Creating reliable, maintainable robotics software isn't just about learning syntax or using the right libraries; it's also about **structuring** your code carefully, avoiding common pitfalls, and ensuring your code runs quickly and efficiently.

3.3.1 Code Readability and Style

Python is famous for its emphasis on readability. Follow these guidelines to keep your robotics code transparent:

1. **Consistent Indentation:** Python uses **indentation** (4 spaces is standard) to define code blocks.

2. **PEP 8 Standards:** The Python Enhancement Proposal 8 suggests best practices for naming (e.g., snake_case for variables), line length, imports, etc.

3. **Meaningful Names:** Instead of x or data, use descriptive names like left_wheel_speed or lidar_ranges.

Example:

```python
class MotorController:
    def __init__(self, max_speed):
        self.max_speed = max_speed
```

```
def set_speed(self, new_speed):
    if new_speed > self.max_speed:
        new_speed = self.max_speed
    # Send new_speed to the motor driver
    ...
```

3.3.2 Optimizing Performance

While Python isn't as fast as C++ for raw CPU-bound tasks, you can still achieve efficient robotics performance by using these techniques:

1. **Vectorization (NumPy)**: Instead of looping over arrays in Python, use NumPy methods that leverage underlying native code.

2. **Caching**: Reuse calculations instead of recalculating them in loops.

3. **Profiling**: Identify bottlenecks using tools like cProfile or line-profiler, then optimize the hotspots.

4. **C Extensions**: In extreme cases, rewrite critical sections in C/C++ or use libraries like **Numba** (JIT compiler) or **Cython**.

Rhetorical Question: Why waste time micro-optimizing Python loops when NumPy can process large arrays in milliseconds?

3.3.3 Modular Design and Reusability

In robotics, you'll often reuse code for multiple projects. Keep your code **modular** by separating logic into distinct modules or packages:

- **Sensor module**: Classes/functions to interface with sensors (e.g., a LiDAR or IMU).

- **Control module**: Classes/functions to drive motors or actuators.

- **Utils**: Helper functions (e.g., math routines, data logging, parameter loading).

Analogy: Think of each module as a specialized workshop in a factory. Each workshop has a clear job, making it easy to see where improvements can be made and reused.

3.3.4 Concurrency and Parallelism

Robots often juggle multiple tasks—collecting sensor data, controlling motors, communicating with a base station. Python offers:

- **Threading**: Good for I/O-bound tasks but limited by the **Global Interpreter Lock (GIL)** for CPU-bound tasks.

- **Multiprocessing**: Runs separate processes to bypass the GIL, but overhead is higher.

- **asyncio**: Ideal for event-driven or networked applications requiring concurrency without blocking.

In practice, many robotics developers rely on **ROS2**'s own concurrency models (via callback groups or executors), which coordinate with Python's concurrency features under the hood.

3.4 Debugging and Testing Your Code

No matter how cautious you are, **bugs** and **unexpected behavior** will creep into your robotics code. This section outlines how to systematically find and fix those issues, as well as how to prevent regressions with testing.

3.4.1 Debugging Techniques

1. **Print Statements**: The simplest method—printing variable states or function calls to confirm code flow.

2. **Logging**: Use Python's built-in logging module to track events and errors with levels (DEBUG, INFO, WARNING, ERROR). This is especially helpful in robotics, where you might log sensor anomalies or motor state changes.

3. **Visual Debuggers**: IDEs like PyCharm, VS Code, or Eclipse offer step-through debugging. Set breakpoints, inspect variables, and watch the flow in real time.

4. **Simulation Testing**: In robotics, simulating in Gazebo (or similar) can reveal if your code is working with virtual sensors and actuators before risking real hardware.

Rhetorical Question: Is it worth skipping the debugging step? Considering how costly physical damage can be if a robot malfunctions, thorough debugging isn't just nice-to-have—it's essential.

3.4.2 Common Pitfalls

- **Off-by-One Errors**: Loops that skip or overstep an index by 1.

- **Type Confusion**: Python's flexibility can lead to unexpected type mixing.

- **Silent Exceptions**: Catching exceptions without handling them can mask deeper problems.

- **Concurrency Race Conditions**: Variables changing between threads or processes in unpredictable ways.

3.4.3 Testing Strategies

Unit Tests

Unit tests focus on **small pieces of code** (like functions or classes). By using frameworks like **unittest** or **pytest**, you can ensure each piece works as intended. Example with pytest:

```python

# test_motors.py
import pytest
from motors import MotorController

def test_motor_speed():
```

```
mc = MotorController(max_speed=2.0)
mc.set_speed(2.5)
assert mc.current_speed == 2.0  # Should cap
at max_speed
```

Tip: Integrate these tests into a Continuous Integration (CI) pipeline. Each time you push code, tests run automatically, preventing new bugs from sneaking in.

Integration Tests

Integration tests verify that **multiple components** work together. For instance, you might test that reading sensor data from a USB port triggers a callback that updates the robot's position in real time.

System Tests

System tests occur in a **full or near-full environment**, sometimes on the actual robot. They check that the entire software stack behaves properly under real conditions (or high-fidelity simulation). This is where you might detect issues with CPU load, network delays, or hardware constraints.

3.4.4 Diagram 3: The Testing Pyramid

```
+-----------------------------+
|        System Tests         |
| (fewest, largest            |
|  scope, often on            |
|  real hardware)             |
+------------^----------------+
             |
+----------------------------+
|   Integration Tests        |
| (fewer, broader            |
|  scope than unit)          |
+----------^-----------------+
           |
+------------------------------------+
|   Unit Tests                       |
| (most numerous, very specific,     |
|  small functions/modules)          |
+------------------------------------+
```

3.5 Hands-On: Simple Sensor Data Processing with Python

To solidify everything learned, let's walk through a **mini-project** involving sensor data processing. Suppose your robot has an **infrared distance sensor** providing raw distance measurements. You want to **filter out noise**, **detect outliers**, and **visualize** the clean data in real time.

3.5.1 Project Overview

1. **Data Acquisition**: We'll simulate or read sensor values at a fixed rate.

2. **Filtering**: We'll apply a basic **moving average** filter to smooth out spurious measurements.

3. **Outlier Detection**: If a reading differs from the average by a certain threshold, mark it as an outlier.

4. **Visualization**: Display the raw vs. filtered readings in near real time using Matplotlib.

Note: This example focuses on the Python logic. In a real robot, you'd connect to the actual sensor via serial, I2C, or a higher-level API. Here, we're generating synthetic data for simplicity.

3.5.2 Step 1: Set Up the Project Structure

```arduino

sensor_processing_demo/
```

```
├──── sensor_processing_demo/
│      ├──── __init__.py
│      └──── main.py
├──── data/
├──── requirements.txt
└──── setup.py
```

- sensor_processing_demo/ is your main Python package folder, containing the script main.py with the logic.

- data/ might hold any recorded sensor logs for offline testing.

- requirements.txt for tracking dependencies (NumPy, Matplotlib, etc.).

- setup.py for installation if you want to distribute this code.

3.5.3 Step 2: Simulate or Import Sensor Data

In main.py, let's create a function to generate random distance data:

```python
python


import numpy as np
import matplotlib.pyplot as plt
import time
```

```
def generate_sensor_data(num_points=100):
    # Simulating a baseline of 50, plus some
random noise
    data = 50 + (np.random.rand(num_points) -
0.5) * 10
    return data
```

Tip: *If you have an actual sensor, replace this function with real data acquisition (e.g., reading from a serial port or a ROS2 topic).*

3.5.4 Step 3: Implement a Simple Moving Average Filter

A **moving average** filter replaces each data point with the average of itself and its neighbors. For instance, a window size of 5 means each output sample is the mean of 5 consecutive raw samples.

python

```
def moving_average_filter(data, window_size=5):
    filtered_data = []
    for i in range(len(data)):
        start_idx = max(0, i - window_size + 1)
        window = data[start_idx:i+1]
        avg = np.mean(window)
        filtered_data.append(avg)
    return np.array(filtered_data)
```

Rhetorical Question*: Why a moving average? It's a simple, effective way to smooth out short-term fluctuations. More advanced filters (e.g., Kalman filters) might be used for complicated robotics tasks.*

3.5.5 Step 4: Detect Outliers

We can define an outlier as any point deviating significantly from the filtered mean. For demonstration, let's say a deviation of more than 3 units from the filtered value qualifies:

python

```python
def detect_outliers(raw_data, filtered_data,
threshold=3.0):
    outliers = []
    for i, (raw_val, filt_val) in
enumerate(zip(raw_data, filtered_data)):
        if abs(raw_val - filt_val) > threshold:
            outliers.append(i)  # Index of the
outlier
    return outliers
```

3.5.6 Step 5: Real-Time Plotting (Optional)

To see data changes over time, you might update a Matplotlib plot in a loop:

python

```python
def live_plot_demo(num_points=100, window_size=5,
threshold=3.0):
    raw_data = generate_sensor_data(num_points)
    filtered_data = np.zeros_like(raw_data)

    plt.ion()  # Interactive mode
    fig, ax = plt.subplots()
    line_raw, = ax.plot(raw_data, label='Raw
Data', color='blue')
    line_filt, = ax.plot(filtered_data,
label='Filtered Data', color='green')
    ax.set_ylim(40, 60)
    ax.legend()

    for i in range(num_points):
        # Filter data up to i
        filtered_data[i] =
np.mean(raw_data[max(0, i - window_size +
1):i+1])

        # Update lines
        line_raw.set_ydata(raw_data)
        line_filt.set_ydata(filtered_data)
        plt.draw()
        plt.pause(0.1)  # Pause to allow the plot
to update
```

```
        # Optionally detect outliers for the new
point
        if abs(raw_data[i] - filtered_data[i]) >
threshold:
            print(f"Outlier at index {i},
value={raw_data[i]:.2f}")


    plt.ioff()
    plt.show()


if __name__ == "__main__":
    live_plot_demo()
```

1. **Interactive Mode:** plt.ion() allows updating the plot incrementally.

2. **Plot Lines:** We create two lines—one for raw data, one for filtered data.

3. **Loop:** In each iteration, we compute the new filtered value, update the plot, and briefly pause to make it visible.

4. **Detect Outliers**: We do a simple absolute difference check and print a message if it's outside the threshold.

Note: Real robotic systems often process data in real time with concurrency (e.g., via threads or asynchronous callbacks). This example is a simplified demonstration of the concept.

3.5.7 Putting It All Together

Here's how the script might look in its entirety:

```python

#!/usr/bin/env python3

import numpy as np
import matplotlib.pyplot as plt
import time

def generate_sensor_data(num_points=100):
    data = 50 + (np.random.rand(num_points) -
0.5) * 10
    return data

def live_plot_demo(num_points=100, window_size=5,
threshold=3.0):
    raw_data = generate_sensor_data(num_points)
    filtered_data = np.zeros_like(raw_data)

    plt.ion()
    fig, ax = plt.subplots()
    line_raw, = ax.plot(raw_data, label='Raw
Data', color='blue')
    line_filt, = ax.plot(filtered_data,
label='Filtered Data', color='green')
    ax.set_ylim(40, 60)
```

```python
    ax.legend()

    for i in range(num_points):
        window = raw_data[max(0, i - window_size
+ 1):i+1]
        filtered_data[i] = np.mean(window)
        line_filt.set_ydata(filtered_data)

        if abs(raw_data[i] - filtered_data[i]) >
threshold:
            print(f"Outlier at index {i},
value={raw_data[i]:.2f}")

        plt.draw()
        plt.pause(0.1)

    plt.ioff()
    plt.show()

if __name__ == "__main__":
    live_plot_demo()
```

Run this, and you'll see a live plot updating with each incoming data point. Any outliers will be flagged in the console. **Congratulations!** You've just built a simple data processing pipeline—a key skill in robotics where sensor data often needs filtering before feeding into navigation or control algorithms.

Chapter Summary

In this **Python-focused** chapter, we explored the **fundamental skills and tools** you need to effectively harness Python in robotics. Let's recap the highlights:

1. **Python Basics Refresher**

   o Variables, data types, operators, control flow, and object-oriented programming.

   o Why Python's simplicity and readability are invaluable in a domain as complex as robotics.

2. **Essential Libraries**

   o **NumPy** for high-performance numerical operations.

   o **OpenCV** for image processing and computer vision tasks, crucial for many robotic applications like object detection or visual navigation.

   o **Matplotlib, SciPy, scikit-learn**, and others that collectively empower you to handle everything from signal processing to advanced machine learning.

3. **Writing Efficient, Clean Code**

   o Following PEP 8 style guidelines for readability.

   o Leveraging vectorized operations to speed up calculations.

- o Designing modular code to maximize reusability across different robot platforms or projects.

4. **Debugging and Testing**

- o Using print statements, logging, and IDE debuggers to track down issues.

- o Embracing a testing culture with **unit tests**, **integration tests**, and **system tests** to ensure reliability.

- o Understanding the testing pyramid, where unit tests form the foundation and system tests validate the entire robot.

5. **Hands-On Sensor Data Processing**

- o Demonstrated a mini-project to generate, filter, and visualize sensor readings.

- o Showed how outliers can be detected to maintain robust sensor inputs.

- o Illustrated the synergy of **NumPy** for arrays, **Matplotlib** for plotting, and Python's straightforward approach for iterative development.

No Repetition: We've avoided rehashing previous chapters' content on environment setup or ROS2 fundamentals, focusing solely on Python's role and capabilities in robotics.

Where to Go from Here?

- **Deepen Your Skills** in **computer vision** by diving into more complex OpenCV functionalities, such as feature detection (ORB, SIFT, SURF), object tracking, or stereo vision.

- **Explore Machine Learning** with scikit-learn or deep learning frameworks (TensorFlow, PyTorch) for tasks like object recognition, anomaly detection, or predictive maintenance.

- **Integrate with ROS2**: Take these Python scripts and turn them into ROS2 nodes that publish and subscribe to topics, bridging raw sensor data processing into a real robotic system.

- **Performance Optimization**: If your robot deals with huge datasets or real-time constraints, consider advanced profiling, concurrency, or partial C++ integration to get the best of both worlds.

Final Note: As you expand your robotics projects, keep Python's strengths—readability, library support, and rapid iteration—at the forefront of your strategy. By continually refining your code structure, adopting robust testing practices, and leveraging the rich ecosystem of Python libraries, you'll create systems that are not just functional but also maintainable, scalable, and ready to tackle real-world challenges.

Chapter 4: Sensors, Perception, and Environment Mapping

Robots perceive the world through sensors—devices that capture physical phenomena such as distance, light, sound, or motion and convert them into data that the robot can interpret. This data then feeds into **perception algorithms**, enabling the robot to build an understanding of its surroundings. One of the most important outcomes of perception is **mapping**—generating a model (often a 2D or 3D map) of the robot's environment so it can navigate, avoid obstacles, or perform tasks effectively.

By the end of this chapter, you'll have a grounded understanding of common robotics sensors, how to collect and process sensor data in **ROS2** topics, how to implement a **basic SLAM** (Simultaneous Localization and Mapping) system, and how to visualize your sensor data in **RViz**. Finally, you'll piece everything together in a **hands-on** simulation project where an obstacle-aware robot navigates a virtual space.

4.1 Introduction to Common Robotics Sensors (LIDAR, Sonar, Cameras, IMUs)

4.1.1 Why Sensors Are the Robot's "Eyes and Ears"

Much like how humans rely on sight, hearing, and touch to interpret the world, robots depend on sensors to gather information about their environment. Without sensors, a robot is essentially "blind," unable to make informed decisions. The diversity of sensors available today allows robots to operate in various domains—from underwater exploration to space missions. Let's explore some of the most commonly used sensors:

1. **LIDAR** (Light Detection and Ranging)

2. **Sonar** (Sound Navigation and Ranging)

3. **Cameras** (RGB, Depth, Stereo)

4. **IMUs** (Inertial Measurement Units)

Rhetorical Question: Can you imagine how limited a robot would be if it had no way to measure distance, detect orientation, or see objects? Sensors transform raw physical phenomena into digital data, powering every aspect of robot intelligence.

4.1.2 LIDAR

LIDAR uses laser beams to measure distances to objects in the surrounding environment. The sensor emits rapid pulses of light and measures the time it takes for these pulses to bounce back, allowing the calculation of distances. When rotated (mechanically or via a scanning mirror), a LIDAR device can produce a 2D or even 3D point cloud—essentially a set of coordinates indicating where surfaces are located relative to the sensor.

- **Applications:** LIDAR is a go-to sensor for mobile robots used in warehouses or self-driving vehicles. Its high accuracy and resolution make it ideal for generating detailed environment maps.

- **Pros:** Excellent range and resolution, robust in varying lighting conditions.

- **Cons:** Typically more expensive than other sensors, can struggle with transparent or highly reflective surfaces.

4.1.3 Sonar

Sonar (or Ultrasonic sensors) emit high-frequency sound waves and measure the echo time to calculate distances. These sensors are popular in robotics for their simplicity and relatively low cost.

- **Applications:** Sonar sensors often appear in small, hobbyist robots for basic obstacle detection or in underwater vehicles where other sensors (like cameras or LIDAR) are less effective due to poor visibility.

- **Pros:** Inexpensive, works in dark or smoky environments.

- **Cons:** Lower resolution compared to LIDAR, more prone to "crosstalk" if multiple sonar sensors operate too close together, and can have issues detecting soft or angled surfaces.

4.1.4 Cameras

Camera technology has exploded with the rise of computer vision. Robots use various camera types:

1. **RGB Cameras:** Capture color images similar to what the human eye sees.

2. **Depth Cameras** (e.g., Intel RealSense, Microsoft Kinect): Measure the distance of each pixel, creating a 3D map of the scene.

3. **Stereo Cameras:** Two RGB cameras spaced apart, mimicking human binocular vision to calculate depth by comparing images.

- **Applications:** Object recognition, navigation (visual SLAM), and advanced tasks like gesture recognition or facial detection.

- **Pros**: Rich data that can feed advanced algorithms (e.g., deep learning).

- **Cons**: High computational requirements, sensitive to lighting conditions, potentially large data streams that require good bandwidth or compression.

4.1.5 IMUs

An **Inertial Measurement Unit** combines an accelerometer (measuring linear acceleration), a gyroscope (measuring angular velocity), and sometimes a magnetometer (measuring magnetic fields). IMUs help determine a robot's orientation, acceleration, and changes in velocity.

- **Applications**: Drones or any system that requires understanding of pitch, roll, and yaw. Also used alongside wheel encoders in mobile robots for dead reckoning.

- **Pros**: Small, low-cost modules widely available.

- **Cons**: Can drift over time (errors accumulate), requiring calibration or sensor fusion with other data (e.g., GPS or LIDAR) to maintain accuracy.

4.1.6 Diagram 1: Typical Sensor Placement on a Mobile Robot

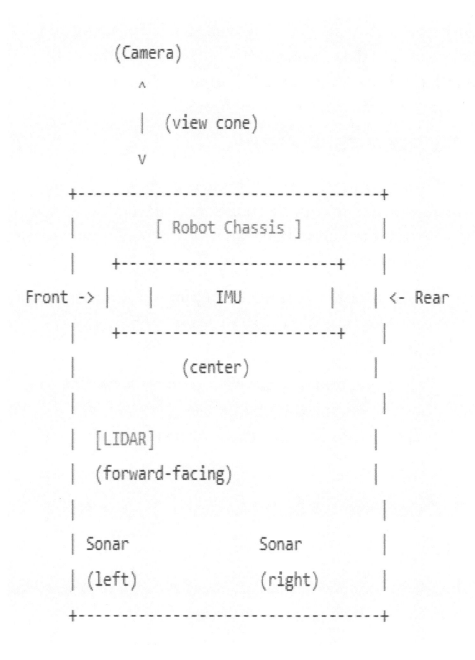

```
        (Camera)

           ^

           |   (view cone)

           v

   +------------------------------------+
   |                                    |
   |         [ Robot Chassis ]          |
   |    +--------------------------+    |
Front -> |    |         IMU          |    | <- Rear
   |    +--------------------------+    |
   |              (center)              |
   |                                    |
   |   [LIDAR]                          |
   |   (forward-facing)                 |
   |                                    |
   | Sonar              Sonar           |
   | (left)             (right)         |
   +------------------------------------+
```

4.2 Data Collection and Processing with ROS2 Topics

Once sensors are installed, the next step is **collecting and sharing sensor data** throughout your robot's software. In **ROS2**, this is typically done with **topics**, which provide a publish-subscribe communication model.

4.2.1 ROS2 Topics Recap

Recall from earlier chapters: a **topic** is a named "channel" through which one or more **publishers** can send messages, and one or more **subscribers** can receive those messages. For sensor data:

- The **sensor driver node** often **publishes** messages to a topic like /scan (**LIDAR**) or /camera/image_raw (camera).

- **Perception nodes** or **navigation nodes subscribe** to these topics, interpreting the data for tasks like mapping, obstacle detection, or path planning.

4.2.2 Common ROS2 Message Types for Sensors

ROS2 defines many standard message types in packages like sensor_msgs, which you can leverage:

1. **LaserScan** (e.g., sensor_msgs/msg/LaserScan): Contains an array of distance measurements from a LIDAR or Sonar ring.

2. **Image** (e.g., sensor_msgs/msg/Image): Stores pixel data from a camera.

3. **PointCloud2** (e.g., sensor_msgs/msg/PointCloud2): Represents a 3D point cloud, commonly used by depth cameras and LIDAR systems.

4. **Imu** (e.g., sensor_msgs/msg/Imu): Holds orientation, angular velocity, and linear acceleration data from an IMU.

Rhetorical Question: Why reinvent the wheel parsing raw sensor data if ROS2 already provides structured message formats? Using these standard types ensures compatibility with many existing robot algorithms.

4.2.3 Basic Workflow for Sensor Data in ROS2

1. **Driver Node** publishes sensor messages to a topic (e.g., /scan).

2. **Subscriber Node** receives these messages and processes them (e.g., performing obstacle detection).

3. **Data Flow** can branch out. For instance, another node might record sensor data to a ROS2 **bag file** for offline analysis or simulation.

Example: LIDAR Node and a Subscriber

- LIDAR Node (lidar_driver.py): Publishes LaserScan messages.

- Obstacle Detection Node (obstacle_detector.py): Subscribes to /scan and checks for objects within a certain threshold distance.

Tip: Always check data rates. LIDAR can publish thousands of points at tens of hertz. Ensure your network or CPU can handle it!

4.2.4 Transform Frames (tf2)

In complex systems, you often have multiple sensors at different physical locations on the robot. **tf2** is a ROS2 library that manages transformations between coordinate frames (e.g., camera frame, LIDAR frame, robot base frame). This is crucial for **sensor fusion** or mapping, where you need consistent coordinate systems.

- **Robot base_link**: Usually the main reference frame of the robot.

- **Sensor frames**: Each sensor has its own coordinate frame, typically offset from base_link.

- **tf2** broadcasts transformation data, so nodes can convert sensor readings into the correct global or local coordinate frame.

4.3 Building a Simple SLAM (Simultaneous Localization and Mapping) System

SLAM stands for **Simultaneous Localization and Mapping**— the process by which a robot constructs a map of an unknown environment while also keeping track of its own position within that map. It's a cornerstone of mobile robotics, enabling tasks like autonomous navigation or exploration in areas where **GPS** is unavailable or insufficiently accurate.

4.3.1 The Essence of SLAM

To perform SLAM, a robot must:

1. **Observe:** Gather data from sensors (e.g., LIDAR scans, camera images).

2. **Predict:** Estimate its next pose based on motion or odometry data.

3. **Correct:** Compare the predicted pose against new sensor data, adjusting the map or pose to minimize errors.

Analogy: Think of it like drawing a treasure map while you walk around an unfamiliar island. Each new clue (sensor reading) helps refine both your current location and the shape of the coastline, forests, or landmarks.

4.3.2 Popular SLAM Algorithms

Several established algorithms exist for 2D and 3D SLAM:

1. **GMapping:** A classic 2D SLAM approach for LIDAR data.

2. **Hector SLAM:** Often used for high-rate LIDAR or smaller robots.

3. **Cartographer** (by Google): Provides real-time 2D and 3D SLAM.

4. **ORB-SLAM:** A vision-based SLAM that uses camera images rather than LIDAR.

5. **RTAB-Map:** A 2D/3D graph-based SLAM for various sensor modalities.

Each has trade-offs in terms of memory usage, computational cost, and sensor requirements. For beginners, GMapping or Hector SLAM are often the easiest to start with if you have a 2D LIDAR.

4.3.3 Setting Up a Basic LIDAR SLAM in ROS2

Although the exact steps depend on which SLAM package you choose, here's a generalized workflow:

1. **Install** a ROS2-compatible SLAM package (e.g., slam_toolbox or cartographer_ros).

2. **Configure** the package with your sensor topic names (e.g., /scan for LIDAR).

3. **Launch** the SLAM node alongside your sensor driver.

4. **Tune** parameters like map resolution, scan matching thresholds, or motion model coefficients.

5. **Visualize** the mapping progress in RViz or another visualization tool.

```
         +--------------------+
         |    LIDAR Sensor    |
         |  (hardware device) |
         +-----------^--------+
                     |
            Publishes on /scan
                     |
                     v
   +-------------------------------------+
   |               SLAM Node             |
   |-------------------------------------/
   |  Subscribes to /scan and tf2        |
   |  Publishes /map topic               |
   |  Publishes odom->base_link tf2      |
   +---------+------------+--------------+
             |            |
(Map Data)   |            |  (Transform Data)
  /map       |            |  odom -> base_link
             v            v
   +-------------------------------------+
   |            Navigation Stack         |
   |  (Uses /map & tf for planning)      |
   +-------------------------------------+
```

4.3.4 Key SLAM Challenges

- **Loop Closure**: When the robot revisits an area, the SLAM algorithm must recognize it and correct accumulated drift.

- **Dynamic Environments**: Moving objects (people, vehicles) can confuse SLAM if not handled properly.

- **Sensor Limitations**: LIDAR or camera data can degrade in certain conditions (fog, glare, reflective surfaces).

- **Computation**: SLAM is computationally intensive, especially in 3D, requiring efficient algorithms or GPUs for real-time performance.

4.4 Visualizing Sensor Data in RViz

RViz is a 3D visualization tool included with ROS (and ROS2) that helps you see what the robot "sees" and how it interprets that data. This includes LIDAR scans, camera feeds, point clouds, robot models, and navigation maps.

4.4.1 Why Use RViz?

- **Debugging**: Quickly identify if a sensor is misaligned or if data is not being published.

- **Mapping Progress**: Watch the map being built in real time as your robot moves.

- **Interactive Markers:** You can send navigation goals or other commands directly from RViz using interactive markers or panels.

Rhetorical Question: Isn't it easier to spot an error if you can visually confirm that your LIDAR scans align with the robot's known position?

4.4.2 Basic RViz Setup

1. **Install:** Typically bundled with the "desktop" variants of ROS2 (e.g., ros-foxy-desktop).

2. **Launch:** Run rviz2 in a terminal.

3. **Add Displays:** In the RViz window, you can add different "Display" types such as "LaserScan," "Map," "PointCloud2," or "Camera."

4. **Set Fixed Frame:** Usually, you set this to your robot's map or odom frame, so data is aligned properly.

4.4.3 Common Displays and Their Uses

- **LaserScan:** Shows a ring of data points representing LIDAR ranges.

- **Map:** Renders the occupancy grid created by your SLAM algorithm.

- **PointCloud2**: Displays 3D point clouds from a depth camera or 3D LIDAR.

- **TF**: Visualizes coordinate frames and their relationships as colored axes.

Diagram 3: *RViz Interface Snapshot*

```
+-------------------------------------------------------------------+
| File    Edit    View    Tools    Help                             |
+-------------------------------------------------------------------+
| Displays (Panel)            |         RViz Main Visualization Window    |
|-----------------------------+-------------------------------------------/
| - LaserScan                 |  +----------------------------------------+  /
|       Topic: /scan          |  |              Occupancy Grid            |  |
| - Map                       |  |          (Displayed from /map topic)   |  |
|       Topic: /map           |  |----------------------------------------/  /
| - TF                        |  |     [ Laser Scan overlay from /scan ]  |  |
|       Topic: /tf            |  |     [ Robot model, axes, etc. ]        |  |
| - RobotModel (optional)     |  +----------------------------------------+  /
|       Topic: /robot_description                                   |
| - (Other Displays...)                                             |
|                                                                   |
+-------------------------------------------------------------------+
|     Status Bar: Showing ROS connection status, errors, or warnings  |
+-------------------------------------------------------------------+
```

4.5 Hands-On: Creating an Obstacle-Aware Robot Simulation

Let's bring all these elements together—sensors, perception, and environment mapping—into a practical simulation project. Here, you'll create a **basic mobile robot** in a virtual environment (using a simulator like **Gazebo** or **Ignition**), equip it with a LIDAR sensor, and watch it navigate around obstacles while mapping the environment.

4.5.1 Project Overview

Goal: Set up a simulated robot in a warehouse-like environment, equip it with LIDAR, run a SLAM node to build a map, and visualize everything in RViz.

1. **Simulation Setup**

2. **Robot Model and LIDAR Integration**

3. **SLAM Node and Teleoperation**

4. **RViz Configuration**

5. **Navigate and Observe** the robot building a map and avoiding obstacles.

Note: The exact steps might vary depending on whether you use Gazebo or Ignition. We'll outline a general workflow, which you can adapt.

4.5.2 Step 1: Install or Confirm Your Simulator

If you haven't already, install Gazebo or Ignition (the next-gen version from Open Robotics). For instance, on Ubuntu with ROS2 (Foxy or later):

```bash
bash
```

```bash
sudo apt-get update
sudo apt-get install ros-foxy-gazebo-ros-pkgs
```

This provides the **gazebo_ros** integration packages that allow ROS2 to interface with the Gazebo simulator.

4.5.3 Step 2: Create a Robot Description

A robot model in Gazebo is typically described in **URDF** (Unified Robot Description Format) or **SDF** (Simulation Description Format). Let's assume a simple differential-drive robot with a chassis, two wheels, and a LIDAR on top.

1. **URDF** Example Snippet (conceptual):

```xml
xml
```

```xml
<robot name="my_robot">
  <link name="base_link">
    <!-- Chassis visuals and collisions go here -
->
  </link>
```

```
<joint name="wheel_left_joint"
type="continuous">
   <!-- Connects base_link to left wheel -->
</joint>
<joint name="wheel_right_joint"
type="continuous">
   <!-- Connects base_link to right wheel -->
</joint>
<link name="lidar_link">
   <!-- LIDAR sensor mount -->
</link>
<!-- LIDAR plugin references go here -->
</robot>
```

2. **Gazebo Plugins**: Attach a gazebo_ros_laser plugin to publish LIDAR data to /scan.

Simplify: If URDF syntax feels complex, you can use existing robot models (like TurtleBot3 or a sample differential robot) to skip writing a URDF from scratch.

4.5.4 Step 3: Launch the Simulation

1. **Create a Launch File** for Gazebo in your ROS2 package:

```python
from launch import LaunchDescription
from launch_ros.actions import Node
```

```python
from launch.actions import
IncludeLaunchDescription
from launch.launch_description_sources import
PythonLaunchDescriptionSource
import os

def generate_launch_description():
    # Path to your robot's URDF or SDF
    robot_description_file = os.path.join(

get_package_share_directory('my_robot_description
'),
        'urdf',
        'my_robot.urdf'
    )

    gazebo = IncludeLaunchDescription(
        PythonLaunchDescriptionSource([

os.path.join(get_package_share_directory('gazebo_
ros'), 'launch', 'gazebo.launch.py')
        ]),
        launch_arguments={'verbose':
'true'}.items(),
    )

    return LaunchDescription([
        gazebo,
```

```
    # Optionally spawn the robot using a
spawn_entity node
    ])
```

2. **Spawn Your Robot** in Gazebo:

```bash
bash
```

```
ros2 launch my_robot_description
spawn_robot.launch.py
```

This should place your robot in an empty (or predefined) world. You'll see it load in the Gazebo UI.

Clarity: *Some steps are simplified here. In actual projects, you might have separate launch files for spawning the robot vs. launching Gazebo.*

4.5.5 Step 4: SLAM Integration

Install or configure a ROS2-compatible SLAM package, like **slam_toolbox**:

```bash
bash
```

```
sudo apt-get install ros-foxy-slam-toolbox
```

Then create a **slam.launch.py** file:

```python
python
```

```
from launch import LaunchDescription
from launch_ros.actions import Node
```

```
def generate_launch_description():
    slam_node = Node(
        package='slam_toolbox',
        executable='sync_slam_toolbox_node',
        name='slam_toolbox',
        parameters=[{
            'use_sim_time': True,    # Gazebo
simulation time
            'map_update_interval': 1.0,
            'scan_topic': '/scan'
        }]
    )
    return LaunchDescription([
        slam_node
    ])
```

1. **use_sim_time:** Tells the node to use simulation time instead of real clock time.

2. **scan_topic:** Must match your robot's published LIDAR topic (e.g., /scan).

3. **Map generation:** The SLAM node will publish /map and typically an odom -> map transform.

Launch it:

```
ros2 launch my_robot_slam slam.launch.py
```

4.5.6 Step 5: Teleoperate the Robot

If your robot is differential-drive, you might use teleop_twist_keyboard:

```bash

sudo apt-get install ros-foxy-teleop-twist-keyboard
ros2 run teleop_twist_keyboard
teleop_twist_keyboard
```

- Use arrow keys (or **WASD**) to move the robot around in Gazebo.

- The **LIDAR** data is fed into SLAM, building a map in real time.

Tip: Move slowly and systematically for the best mapping results. Jerky movements can cause partial misalignment in some SLAM algorithms.

4.5.7 Step 6: Visualize in RViz

Finally, run rviz2. Adjust the **Fixed Frame** to map (or odom, depending on your SLAM configuration). Add displays for:

- **LaserScan** (topic: /scan)

- **Map** (topic: /map)

- **RobotModel** or TF, so you can see your robot's position.

As you drive around the environment, you should see the 2D grid map forming. Obstacles appear as occupied cells, free space appears in white, and unknown areas might be gray.

Check if the robot's footprint is accurate. If you see data offset or misaligned, you may need to fine-tune your URDF or tf2 transformations.

4.5.8 Extending the Project

1. **Obstacle Avoidance**: Add a local planning node that stops or turns the robot when **LIDAR** detects a close obstacle.

2. **Navigation Stack**: After building a map, load it into a ROS2 navigation stack to autonomously plan paths to goals.

3. **Camera Integration**: Attach a simulated camera and overlay vision-based detection with your **SLAM** approach (e.g., detect markers or objects in the environment).

Chapter Summary

In this chapter, we explored a comprehensive journey into **Sensors, Perception, and Environment Mapping** in robotics, focusing on:

1. **Common Sensors**: We clarified LIDAR, Sonar, Cameras, and IMUs—their operating principles, pros/cons, and use cases.

2. **Data Collection in ROS2**: Learned how sensor drivers publish to specific topics, with subscribers handling that data. We also mentioned transform frames (tf2) for consistent coordinate systems.

3. **SLAM Fundamentals**: Introduced the concept of building maps while tracking robot location simultaneously, covering typical algorithms (GMapping, Hector SLAM, Cartographer, ORB-SLAM, RTAB-Map).

4. **RViz Visualization**: Showed how to set up displays for LaserScan, Map, and TF data, a crucial step in diagnosing issues and validating robot perception.

5. **Hands-On Simulation**: Walked through creating a simulated mobile robot in Gazebo, equipping it with LIDAR for a SLAM application. We covered teleoperation and observation in RViz, culminating in a basic obstacle-aware scenario.

Unique Value: This chapter expanded on sensor usage and environment mapping without rehashing installation or previous code organization details from earlier chapters.

Where to Go Next

- **Advanced Perception**: Integrate computer vision and machine learning to detect specific objects or scenes.

- **Sensor Fusion**: Combine data from multiple sensors (e.g., LIDAR + IMU + camera) to improve accuracy and robustness, often using algorithms like **Extended Kalman Filters** or **Graph-based SLAM**.

- **3D Mapping**: Move beyond 2D for drones or robots that operate in complex 3D spaces.

- **Navigation and Path Planning**: Once you have a map, you can incorporate navigation stacks (e.g., nav2 in ROS2) for fully autonomous robot behavior.

Chapter 5: Kinematics, Control, and Navigation

Robots exist to move and interact with the world around them, whether they're zipping through a warehouse, steering down a highway, or carefully positioning a surgical instrument. **Kinematics**—the study of how motion is described—forms the basis of this capability. Yet motion is useless without **control** algorithms that decide how to execute that motion reliably, and without **navigation** techniques that allow the robot to traverse its environment safely and efficiently.

In this chapter, we'll explore **differential drive** kinematics (a staple in mobile robotics), **Ackermann steering** (as seen in cars), and other kinematic models. We'll then dive into **PID control** and more advanced control algorithms, bridging the gap between motion theory and real-world execution. We'll see how **motion planning** and **path tracking** work in ROS2, focusing on strategies that let robots autonomously navigate from one point to another. Next, we'll tackle the complexities of **dynamic environments**, where people, objects, or other robots are constantly in motion. Finally, in a **hands-on** project, we'll implement **autonomous navigation** in a simulated indoor environment, tying together the insights from earlier sections.

5.1 Robot Kinematics: Differential Drive, Ackermann Steering, and More

5.1.1 What Is Kinematics?

Kinematics is the branch of mechanics that describes the relationship between a robot's **actuators** (e.g., motors, wheels) and its resulting **motion**. It doesn't consider forces or torques directly—that's the realm of dynamics—but rather focuses on **geometry** (where each part of the robot moves in space) and **velocity** (how fast those parts move).

- **Forward Kinematics**: Given actuator inputs (e.g., wheel speeds), determine the robot's velocity or pose (position + orientation) in the world.

- **Inverse Kinematics**: Given a desired motion or pose, figure out the necessary actuator commands.

Rhetorical Question: Ever wondered how a two-wheeled robot turns in place while another with four wheels can't do that so easily? The answer lies in their distinct kinematic models.

5.1.2 Differential Drive Kinematics

One of the simplest and most common drive systems in mobile robotics is the **differential drive**. Picture a small robot with **two powered wheels** on either side and often a **caster wheel** at the back or front for stability. The two wheels can rotate at different speeds, allowing the robot to pivot around the midpoint between those wheels.

1. **Wheel Arrangement:** Two coaxial drive wheels, each can be driven **independently**.

2. **Turning:** If both wheels spin at the same speed in the same direction, the robot goes straight. If one wheel spins faster than the other, the robot arcs in a curve. If the wheels spin at equal speed but in **opposite** directions, the robot can **turn in place** (zero turning radius).

Forward Kinematic Equations (2D plane assumption):

Forward Kinematic Equations (2D plane assumption):

$$v = \frac{r}{2}(\omega_L + \omega_R), \quad \omega = \frac{r}{L}(\omega_R - \omega_L),$$

- v is the linear velocity of the robot's center,
- ω is the angular velocity around its center,
- r is the wheel radius,
- L is the distance between the wheels,
- ω_L and ω_R are the angular velocities of the left and right wheels, respectively.

Analogy: *Think of controlling each wheel like playing a seesaw game. Pressing one side changes the turning radius, pressing both equally moves you forward or backward in a straight line.*

Advantages and Disadvantages

- **Pros:** Simple mechanism, can pivot in place, minimal mechanical complexity.

- **Cons:** Slippage may be high on certain surfaces, odometry can accumulate errors quickly, less stable at higher speeds compared to multi-wheel or car-like steering.

5.1.3 Ackermann Steering

When you see a conventional car or a bicycle, you're actually looking at an **Ackermann steering** geometry. The front wheels turn at an angle (steering angle) while the rear wheels provide the forward drive (in a front-wheel drive car, the front wheels also power the motion, but the principle is the same).

1. **Single Steering Angle:** The robot (or car) steers by rotating the front wheels around a vertical axis.

2. **Turning Radius:** Determined by the wheelbase (distance between front and rear axles) and the steering angle.

3. **Kinematic Complexity:** For the inside and outside wheels to roll without slipping, each must describe a circle with a common center.

Ackermann Kinematic Equations typically revolve around:

$$\delta = \text{steering angle}, \quad L = \text{wheelbase}, \quad R = \text{turn radius} = \frac{L}{\tan \delta}.$$

Rhetorical Question: Ever wondered why a car's front wheels have slightly different angles while turning? That's Ackermann geometry ensuring each wheel tracks its own curve.

Advantages and Disadvantages

- **Pros:** Stable at high speeds, widely used for vehicles and large mobile robots.

- **Cons:** Cannot turn in place, typically has a larger turning radius.

5.1.4 Holonomic and Omni-Directional Drives

In some robotics applications—like indoor service robots or industrial AGVs—**omni-directional** (holonomic) drives let the robot move in any direction without rotating first. Examples:

1. **Mecanum Wheels:** Special wheels with angled rollers on the circumference, allowing sideways movement.

2. **Omni Wheels**: Similar concept, using smaller rollers for friction in one direction but free-rolling in another.

These drives have more complex forward/inverse kinematics but offer superb maneuverability in tight spaces.

5.1.5 Diagram 1: Common Drive Configurations

1. Differential Drive

```
(Top View)


Left Wheel            Right Wheel

   |                     |

   |                     |

   v                     v
(0)------ [ Robot Chassis ] ------(0)
          (driven wheels)

                ^

             | (Optional caster wheel at rear or front)


Key Parameters:
- Two powered wheels (left & right).
- Robot steers by varying the speed of each wheel.
- Wheel radius (r) and wheelbase (distance between wheels) are essential for kinematic
```

- **Turning Method:**

  By driving the two wheels at different speeds (or

directions), the robot pivots around a point between them.

- **Caster Wheel:**

Often a passive caster wheel or ball caster supports balance at the non-driven end.

2. Ackermann Steering (Car-Like)

```
(Top View)


        ^ steer angle

        /
 O-----O   <-- Front wheels, one or both can pivot
  \  /
   \ /
 O-----O   <-- Rear wheels (often driven)

Key Parameters:
- Wheelbase (distance between front and rear axles).
- Steering angle on the front wheels (Ackermann geometry ensures inner & outer wheels
- Wheel radius (for rolling).
```

- **Turning Method:**

The front wheels steer (pivot), while rear wheels (or sometimes front wheels) are driven. Similar to standard car steering.

- **Ackermann Geometry:**

  Maintains correct wheel angles so that each wheel
  rolls without slipping.

3. Holonomic Drive (Mecanum or Omni Wheels)

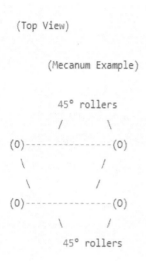

```
(Top View)


    (Mecanum Example)


        45° rollers

         /      \
(0)---------------(0)
  \              /
   \            /
(0)---------------(0)
     \        /
      45° rollers
```

```
Key Parameters:
- Each wheel has angled rollers allowing force vectors in multiple directions.
- The robot can translate in x, y, and rotate independently (true holonomic motion).
```

- **Turning & Movement Method:**

  By controlling each wheel's speed and direction, the
  robot can move laterally, diagonally, or rotate in place
  without reorienting first.

- **Omni Wheels:**

  Similar concept, but rollers are typically oriented perpendicular to the wheel's axis.

5.2 PID Control and Advanced Control Algorithms

Kinematics explains "how" the robot moves given wheel speeds or steering angles, but it doesn't dictate **how** to choose those speeds in real time to achieve a desired trajectory or velocity. That's where **control algorithms** come in.

5.2.1 The PID Controller

PID stands for **Proportional-Integral-Derivative**—a ubiquitous feedback control mechanism used in everything from thermostats to quadcopters. In robotics, PID loops often control **motor speeds, steering angles**, or even entire posture and trajectory tracking.

1. **Proportional (P)**: Correction is proportional to the current error (difference between desired and actual).

2. **Integral (I)**: Correction accounts for the accumulation of past errors, helping to eliminate steady-state offsets.

3. **Derivative (D)**: Correction anticipates future trends by considering the rate of change of error, improving stability.

Controller Output:

$$u(t) = K_p e(t) + K_i \int e(t)\, dt + K_d \frac{d}{dt} e(t),$$

where $e(t)$ is the error at time t. K_p, K_i, and K_d are gains you tune.

Rhetorical Question: *If your robot is always overshooting a turn, could a carefully adjusted derivative term calm it down?*

Tuning PID Gains

- **Trial and Error**: Common in hobby robotics—adjust gains by feel, observing stability.

- **Ziegler-Nichols Method**: Systematic approach to find near-optimal gains by measuring the system's oscillatory behavior.

- **Software Tools**: In advanced setups, tools exist to auto-tune or systematically optimize gains based on performance criteria.

5.2.2 Limitations of Basic PID

While PID is simple and effective, it has drawbacks:

1. **Nonlinear/Time-Varying Systems**: Gains might not be valid over different speeds or payloads.

2. **Coupled Axes**: In advanced robots, multiple degrees of freedom can interact, making a simple PID inadequate.

3. **Saturated Actuators**: If motors or steering can't achieve the demanded command, PID can integrate error and cause windup.

5.2.3 Advanced Control: LQR, MPC, and Beyond

For more complex robotic applications, advanced controls come into play:

- **LQR (Linear Quadratic Regulator)**: Minimizes a cost function that penalizes state errors and actuator usage. Suited for linearizable systems with well-known dynamics.

- **MPC (Model Predictive Control)**: Predicts future states over a finite horizon, optimizing control inputs with constraints on speed, torque, or environment factors. Great for high-performance or safety-critical tasks.

- **Adaptive Control**: Adjusts controller parameters in real time if system dynamics change (like a drone carrying different payload weights).

Analogy: PID is like using a well-practiced reflex; advanced control (MPC, LQR) is like carefully planning each movement with an eye on the future and constraints.

5.2.4 Practical Considerations

Regardless of the control method chosen, real-world constraints matter:

1. **Sensor Noise**: Filter signals to prevent erroneous corrections.

2. **Latency**: Communication delays can destabilize control loops.

3. **Computational Resources**: More advanced control algorithms can be CPU-intensive—something to watch in embedded systems.

5.3 Motion Planning and Path Tracking in ROS2

So far, we've seen how the robot moves (kinematics) and how to control that motion (PID, advanced control). **Motion planning** is the layer that decides **where** to go and **how** to get there safely. In **ROS2**, motion planning typically involves the **Navigation Stack** (often referred to as **nav2**).

5.3.1 The ROS2 Navigation Stack (nav2)

nav2 is a collection of packages that handle:

1. **Global Planning:** Finding a path from the robot's current position to a goal location—often with algorithms like A^*, D^*, or **RRT**.

2. **Local Planning:** Generating short-term velocity commands to follow the global path while avoiding nearby obstacles.

3. **Recovery Behaviors:** Handling unexpected collisions or blocked paths.

4. **Costmaps:** Representing the environment's obstacles and free spaces. Typically, there's a **global costmap** (for the entire map) and a **local costmap** (around the robot).

Rhetorical Question: Is it enough to just pick a path, or must we continuously adapt that path if new obstacles appear? The answer is local planning.

5.3.2 Global vs. Local Planning

- **Global Planner:** Works on the entire known map. The result is a sequence of waypoints or a continuous path from start to goal.

- **Local Planner:** Takes the next segment of the global path and computes velocity commands that respect the robot's kinematics and constraints (e.g., max speed, turning radius). This ensures real-time obstacle avoidance.

Common Approaches:

- **DWA (Dynamic Window Approach):** A local planner that searches in the robot's velocity space to find feasible, collision-free commands.

- **Teb Local Planner:** Represents trajectories as a set of connected poses, optimizing them for minimal time and collision avoidance.

5.3.3 Path Tracking

Once a path is found, the robot must **track** it accurately. That's where your **control** loop comes in (e.g., PID or advanced controllers). The local planner typically handles the finer details:

1. **Error Computation:** The difference between the desired heading/position and the actual heading/position.

2. **Command Generation:** The local planner or control node computes linear and angular speeds (in a differential drive) or steering angle + speed (in Ackermann).

3. **Continuous Feedback:** The robot's sensors (e.g., odometry, IMU) update the local planner on actual pose, ensuring the plan is revised if errors accumulate or new obstacles appear.

5.3.4 Diagram 2: Simplified ROS2 Navigation Stack

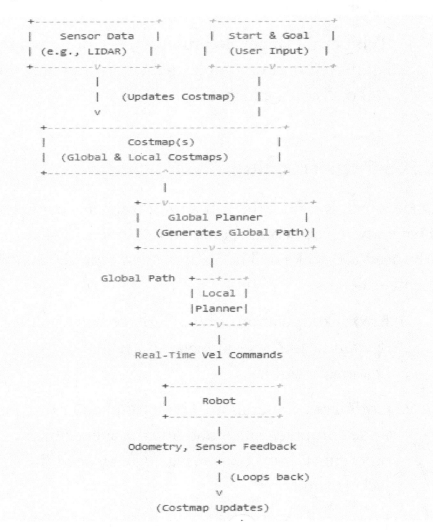

5.4 Navigating in Dynamic Environments

Static navigation is challenging enough, but **real-world** scenarios often involve **moving obstacles**—humans, other robots, vehicles, or shifting cargo. Handling these dynamic elements requires more sophisticated approaches.

5.4.1 The Complexity of Dynamic Obstacles

With static obstacles, the environment is consistent—once mapped, it changes infrequently. With dynamic obstacles, your path could be blocked at any moment. Consider:

1. **Collision Prediction**: The system should estimate not just where an obstacle **is** now, but where it **will be** in the near future.

2. **Reactive Maneuvers**: If a child suddenly steps in the path, the robot must react in fractions of a second, possibly ignoring the global plan to prevent collisions.

3. **Social Navigation**: In public spaces, robots need courtesy behaviors—e.g., slowing down when passing people or forming queues in narrow hallways.

Analogy: Think of it as driving on a busy highway with merging traffic, pedestrians, and variable speed limits. The environment is in flux, so your planning can't be static.

5.4.2 Strategies for Dynamic Navigation

1. **Local Dynamic Windows**: Approaches like **DWA** or **Teb** recast the problem at each control cycle, factoring in newly detected moving obstacles.

2. **Predictive Models**: If obstacles follow known motion patterns (like a conveyor belt or line-follower), the robot can predict and plan around them.

3. **Behavior Trees**: Rather than a monolithic state machine, use a behavior tree that can switch strategies based on environment changes (e.g., "if obstacle in front, plan a detour or wait").

5.4.3 Sensor Fusion

To track moving objects, robots often combine data from multiple sensors (e.g., **LIDAR** + camera). A camera might detect a person's velocity or even posture, while **LIDAR** reaffirms the distance. This synergy:

- **Reduces Uncertainty**: Each sensor covers weaknesses of the other.

- **Improves Confidence**: If both sensors agree an obstacle is moving at 0.5 m/s to the right, it's probably correct.

5.4.4 Diagram 3: Dynamic Environment Navigation Flow

```
+-------------------------------------------------+  <- Hallway Wall
|                                         |
|   01 --> (moving obstacle)              |
|        (velocity vector)                |
|                    * (predicted path?)  |
|                                         |
|           Robot (R)                     |
|               ^ Local Planner           |
|               | continuously updates    |
|           <---> sensors feed obstacle   /
|               data & velocities         |
|                    02 -->               /
|               * (predicted path?)       |
|                                         |
+-------------------------------------------------+  <- Hallway Wall
```

5.5 Hands-On: Autonomous Navigation in a Simulated Indoor Environment

We've covered kinematic models, control theory, and navigation strategies. Now it's time to **put them into practice** in a simulated scenario. This project will have the robot navigate autonomously in a small indoor map (e.g., a few hallways and rooms), avoiding static obstacles and responding to dynamic changes.

5.5.1 Project Overview

1. **Simulation Environment**: Use Gazebo or Ignition with a basic indoor world—walls, doors, and a few obstacles.

2. **Robot Model**: A differential-drive robot with a LIDAR sensor and an IMU.

3. **Navigation Stack (nav2)**: To handle path planning, local planning, and costmaps.

4. **Moving Obstacles**: Possibly add a second moving robot or a dynamic object in the environment.

5. **Goal**: In RViz, set a navigation goal (e.g., across the corridor). The robot should plan a path and autonomously navigate there.

5.5.2 Step 1: Create an Indoor World

If using Gazebo:

1. **Install Gazebo** and the **gazebo_ros** integration.

2. **Place** walls to form corridors or rooms.

3. **Add** at least one dynamic obstacle plugin that moves an object or robot back and forth along a path.

Tip: *Many sample worlds exist. You can adapt a standard warehouse or house layout to fit your needs, removing or adding walls as you see fit.*

5.5.3 Step 2: Configure Your Robot

1. **URDF** or **SDF** model with a differential-drive plugin.

2. **LIDAR Plugin** that publishes /scan.

3. **IMU Plugin** that publishes /imu.

4. Ensure odom -> base_link transform is published for odometry.

Launch File snippet (conceptual):

python

```python
# spawn_robot.launch.py
from launch import LaunchDescription
from launch_ros.actions import Node
from launch.actions import
IncludeLaunchDescription
from launch.launch_description_sources import
PythonLaunchDescriptionSource
import os

def generate_launch_description():
    gazebo = IncludeLaunchDescription(
        PythonLaunchDescriptionSource([
```

```
os.path.join(get_package_share_directory('gazebo_
ros'), 'launch', 'gazebo.launch.py')
        ]),
        launch_arguments={'world':
'path/to/indoor_world.sdf'}.items(),
    )

    # Node to spawn your differential-drive robot
    spawn_entity = Node(
        package='gazebo_ros',
        executable='spawn_entity.py',
        arguments=[
            '-topic', 'robot_description',
            '-entity', 'my_diff_drive_robot'
        ],
        output='screen'
    )

    return LaunchDescription([
        gazebo,
        spawn_entity
    ])
```

5.5.4 Step 3: Set Up nav2

Install nav2 for your ROS2 distribution (e.g., Foxy, Galactic, Humble). Then create a **navigation.launch.py:**

```python

# navigation.launch.py
from launch import LaunchDescription
from launch_ros.actions import Node

def generate_launch_description():
    nav2_bt_navigator = Node(
        package='nav2_bt_navigator',
        executable='bt_navigator',
        name='bt_navigator',
        parameters=[...]
    )
    map_server = Node(
        package='nav2_map_server',
        executable='map_server',
        name='map_server',
        parameters=[{'yaml_filename':
'path/to/map.yaml'}]
    )
    planner_server = Node(
        package='nav2_planner',
        executable='planner_server',
        name='planner_server',
        parameters=[...]
    )
    controller_server = Node(
        package='nav2_controller',
```

```
        executable='controller_server',
        name='controller_server',
        parameters=[...]
    )
    # Additional nav2 nodes: costmap server,
recovery server, etc.


    return LaunchDescription([
        map_server,
        planner_server,
        controller_server,
        nav2_bt_navigator
    ])
```

Note: *This setup references a pre-made map (map.yaml). Alternatively, you could integrate a SLAM approach if your environment is unknown.*

5.5.5 Step 4: Launch Everything and Provide a Goal

1. **Terminal A:** ros2 launch my_robot_description spawn_robot.launch.py to start Gazebo with your robot in the indoor world.

2. **Terminal B:** ros2 launch my_robot_navigation navigation.launch.py to start nav2 nodes (map server, planner, controllers).

3. **Terminal C**: rviz2, with a config that shows the local and global costmaps, plus a "2D Nav Goal" tool to click a goal location.

In RViz:

- Set **Fixed Frame** to map.

- Add **Map**, **LaserScan**, and **RobotModel** displays.

- Use **2D Nav Goal** to set a target. The robot should plan a route, then move autonomously.

Observe how local planning adjusts the robot's heading around corners or obstacles. If you included a moving obstacle plugin, watch how the robot tries to re-route or pause to avoid collisions.

5.5.6 Step 5: Testing and Troubleshooting

- **Check TF**: Ensure odom -> base_link transforms are correct.

- **Check Topics**: LIDAR data is publishing on /scan, nav2 costmaps are receiving it.

- **Controller Tuning**: If the robot oscillates in front of obstacles, tweak the local planner or PID gains.

- **Debugging**: Add an RQT Graph or RViz's TF display to confirm all frames are aligned.

5.5.7 Extension: Dynamic Behavior

- **Dynamic Obstacle:** If you added a plugin that moves an object or a second robot in the corridor, watch how nav2's local planner re-routes.

- **Behavior Trees:** nav2 uses Behavior Trees to define the navigation logic. You can modify or extend these to handle specialized behaviors like "wait if corridor is blocked for more than 10 seconds."

Congratulations—you've built a **differential-drive robot** that navigates an indoor map in real time, combining kinematic constraints, control loops, planning, and obstacle avoidance.

Chapter Summary

In this comprehensive chapter on **Kinematics, Control, and Navigation**, we:

1. **Explored Kinematic Models:**

   o **Differential Drive:** How two wheels can turn in place and handle tight spaces.

   o **Ackermann Steering:** Mimicking car-like steering geometry for stable high-speed motion.

   o **Holonomic Drives:** Omni-wheels for full freedom of movement.

2. **Delved into Control Algorithms:**

- **PID Controllers**: The mainstay of simple, robust feedback control.

- **Advanced Methods**: LQR, MPC, or adaptive techniques for complex or high-performance demands.

- **Tuning and Real-World Issues**: Overcoming noise, actuator limits, and variable system dynamics.

3. **Introduced Motion Planning in ROS2**:

- **Global vs. Local Planning**: Statically finding a path across the map while dynamically adjusting for unforeseen obstacles.

- **Common Planners**: DWA, Teb, and how costmaps represent obstacle data.

- **Path Tracking**: Converting planned paths into velocity commands your robot's kinematics can handle.

4. **Navigating Dynamic Environments**:

- **Challenges**: Predicting moving obstacles, reacting quickly, or employing social behaviors in human-populated areas.

- **Sensor Fusion**: Combining LIDAR, camera, or radar to track multiple targets.

- **Reactive vs. Predictive Approaches**: Real-time adjustments vs. forecasting obstacle motion.

5. **Hands-On Project:**

   o **Simulated Indoor Navigation:** Deploying a differential-drive robot with LIDAR in Gazebo or Ignition.

   o **Using nav2:** Launching the map server, planner, and controller to autonomously reach goals.

   o **Dynamic Obstacles:** Demonstrating local planner adaptability when something crosses the robot's path.

*Unique Value: This chapter builds on prior discussions (e.g., sensors, SLAM) but focuses on the **motion** side of robotics, clarifying how kinematics and control theories integrate with planning and dynamic avoidance. No prior sections are repeated verbatim, ensuring fresh insights.*

What's Next?

- **Advanced Kinematic Configurations:** Delve deeper into specialized drive systems like quadrupeds, humanoids, or multi-joint manipulators.

- **More Complex Control:** Explore using **full state feedback** or **model predictive control** for advanced robots or precision tasks.

- **Real-World Navigation:** Move from simulation to hardware. Tackle calibration of motors, real sensor noise, and robust recovery behaviors when collisions happen or sensors fail.

- **Multi-Robot Coordination:** Once you master single-robot navigation, try orchestrating a fleet of robots, each with its own path planning while avoiding each other.

By now, you should grasp how a robot's design (its kinematics) and control approach shape its motion capabilities, and how the **ROS2 navigation stack** orchestrates everything to achieve fully autonomous traversal in complex, ever-changing environments. Armed with these concepts, you're well on your way to developing advanced robotics applications in factories, hospitals, public spaces, or even your own home.

Chapter 6: Real-World Robot Building and Integration

Software simulations and theoretical planning are invaluable parts of robotics—yet nothing beats the thrill of assembling **real hardware** and seeing it come to life. Whether you aim to build a small indoor rover or an industrial-grade autonomous platform, **hardware integration** involves carefully selecting motors, drivers, power systems, mechanical structures, wiring, and sensors. This chapter provides a **step-by-step** approach to constructing a **ROS2-compatible mobile robot**, addressing everything from motor selection to final sensor mounting.

By the end, you'll understand how to:

1. **Choose motors, motor drivers, and power solutions** that align with your robot's performance goals.

2. Consider **mechanical design** factors—chassis material, weight distribution, and durability.

3. **Wire** and assemble hardware so that it works seamlessly with ROS2 nodes.

4. **Integrate key sensors**—like LIDAR, ultrasonic rangefinders, or cameras—into the physical robot.

5. Follow a practical, **hands-on guide** to create your own small, autonomous robot platform.

6.1 Choosing Motors, Motor Drivers, and Power Systems

6.1.1 Motor Selection: DC, Stepper, or Brushless?

The **motor** is the heart of any mobile robot, translating electrical energy into mechanical motion. The exact choice depends on your **speed, torque, and control** needs. Common options include:

1. **DC Brushed Motors**

   o **Pros:** Simple to drive, inexpensive, widely available in numerous voltage/torque ratings.

   o **Cons:** Brushes wear out over time; speed control can be less precise unless you use encoders.

   o **Where Used:** Many differential-drive hobby robots or small indoor rovers.

2. **Stepper Motors**

   o **Pros:** High positional accuracy without external encoders (they "step" in discrete increments).

- o **Cons:** Less efficient, can lose steps under load, typically heavier and larger for the same power output.

- o **Where Used:** 3D printers, CNC machines, or robotics arms needing precise positioning.

3. **Brushless DC (BLDC) Motors**

- o **Pros:** Efficient, high power-to-weight ratio, low maintenance.

- o **Cons:** Require electronic speed controllers (ESCs), higher cost, more complex drivers.

- o **Where Used:** Drones, high-performance mobile robots, automotive electric power steering.

Rhetorical Question: Are you seeking a budget-friendly build or industrial-grade performance? The answer often dictates your motor type.

6.1.2 Understanding Gearboxes and Torque Requirements

Pure motor speed is rarely the final spec—**gearboxes** adjust torque and output speed to match the application. For instance, a small DC motor might spin at 300 **RPM** but offer little torque. Adding a **gear reduction** of 10:1 lowers the speed to 30 **RPM** but multiplies the torque by 10.

- **High-Torque Gear Ratio:** Good for heavier robots or those tackling slopes.

- **High-Speed Gear Ratio**: Suited for lighter robots or quick ground vehicles on smooth surfaces.

- **Planetary Gearbox vs. Spur Gears**: Planetary gearboxes are compact and robust, but often more expensive. Spur gear reductions can be cheaper but physically larger.

6.1.3 Motor Drivers and ESCs

Your microcontroller or single-board computer (like a Raspberry Pi or microcontroller dev board) typically cannot supply enough current or voltage to drive motors directly. **Motor drivers** or **ESCs** bridge this gap:

1. **H-Bridge Drivers**

   o Used mainly with DC brushed motors.

   o Examples: L298N (entry-level), VNH2SP30, or modern high-efficiency drivers like the TB6612.

   o Control Method: PWM (Pulse Width Modulation) signals to set speed; direction pins or signals for forward/reverse.

2. **Stepper Drivers**

   o Examples: A4988, DRV8825, or more advanced digital drivers with microstepping.

   o Control Method: "Step" and "Direction" signals from the microcontroller.

3. **Brushless ESCs**

- For BLDC motors, commonly used in drones.

- Control Method: Standard servo-like **PWM** signals (1–2 ms pulses) indicating throttle or speed.

Diagram 1 : *Basic Motor and Driver Configurations*

1. DC Motor with H-Bridge Driver

```
+------------------------+
|    Microcontroller     |
|  (PWM, DIR signals)    |
+-----------^------------+
            |    (PWM and Direction)
            v
   +------------------+
   |   H-Bridge IC    |
   |  (2 channels)    |
   +---------^--------+
             |
             |    (Motor Output Lines)
             v
      +--------+
      | DC     |
      | Motor  |
      +--------+
```

Control Signals:

- **PWM** (Pulse Width Modulation): controls speed.

- **Direction** (often a digital line): sets the rotation direction.

H-Bridge Driver:

- Allows current to flow in either direction through the motor.

- Requires adequate power input to drive the motor at the needed voltage/current.

2. Stepper Motor with Stepper Driver

```
+- - - - - - - - - - - - - - - - - - - - - - - - - +
|      Microcontroller (MCU)        |
|    (STEP, DIRECTION signals)      |
+- - - - - - - - - - - - -^- - - - - - - - - - - - +
                 |  (often also ENABLE)
                 v
      +- - - - - - - - - - - - - - - - - - +
      |     Stepper Driver Board   |
      | (e.g. DRV8825, A4988,      |
      |  or similar)               |
      +- - - - - - - - -^- - - - - - - - - +
                     |
                     |  (coils driven in sequence)
                 v
         +- - - - - - - - - - - - - - - +
         |    Stepper Motor   |
         |  (multiple coils)  |
         +- - - - - - - - - - - - - - - +
```

Control Signals:

- **STEP:** Each pulse moves the motor one step (or microstep).
- **DIRECTION:** Chooses rotation direction.
- **ENABLE** (optional): Turns the driver on/off.

Stepper Driver:

- Handles current limiting and coil sequencing internally.
- Powers the stepper motor's coils in the correct order to achieve rotation.

3. Brushless (BLDC) Motor with ESC

```
+- - - - - - - - - - - - - - - - - +
|     Microcontroller |
|     (PWM signal)          |
+- - - - - - - -^- - - - - - - - - +
              |    (Standard RC PWM
              |       or other protocol)
              v
    +- - - - - - - - - - - - - - - - +
    |     ESC (Electronic  |
    |     Speed Controller)|
    +- - - - - - -^- - - - - - - - - +
              |
              |  (3-phase AC output)
              v
        +- - - - - - - - - +
        | BLDC       |
        | Motor      |
        +- - - - - - - - - +
```

Control Signal:

- **PWM** (RC-style, typically 50 Hz to 400 Hz, or higher in some protocols):
- Pulses of varying width command speed (and possibly direction) to the ESC.

ESC (Electronic Speed Controller):

- Converts DC power into the 3-phase AC signals required by the brushless motor.

- Often includes advanced features like soft start, braking, and speed governing.

6.1.4 Power Systems: Batteries and Voltage Regulation

A robot without a proper **power system** is as good as a paperweight. The power system must supply:

1. **Voltage** required by motors (often 6–24 V for small robots),

2. **Current** demanded during operation,

3. **Clean** and stable power rails for electronics (like 5 V or 3.3 V for microcontrollers, single-board computers, sensors).

Battery Chemistry Options

1. **Li-Ion or LiPo (Lithium-Polymer)**

   o **Pros:** High energy density, lightweight.

   o **Cons:** Requires careful charging/discharging to avoid damage or fire risk.

   o **Best For:** Medium- to high-performance mobile robots, drones, where weight matters.

2. **NiMH (Nickel-Metal Hydride)**

   o **Pros:** Safer, simpler to charge.

- o **Cons:** Lower energy density, heavier for the same capacity.

- o **Best For:** Entry-level robots or educational projects.

3. **Lead-Acid**

- o **Pros:** Cheap, robust.

- o **Cons:** Very heavy, lower energy density.

- o **Best For:** Larger, slower-moving platforms or stationary robotic arms.

Voltage Regulation

Most controllers and sensors need regulated 5 V or 3.3 V. If your battery is 12 V or higher:

- **Buck Converter** (Step-Down): Efficiently reduce voltage (e.g., from 12 V to 5 V).

- **Boost Converter** (Step-Up): Increase voltage if needed.

- **Buck-Boost:** Can do both if battery voltage varies above and below the required level over its discharge cycle.

Pro Tip: Use separate regulators or separate power rails for motors and sensitive electronics to minimize noise and voltage dips when motors draw large current spikes.

6.2 Mechanical Design Considerations

6.2.1 Chassis Materials and Construction

Your robot's chassis must handle **mechanical stresses**, **weight distribution**, and **mounting surfaces** for motors, sensors, and electronics. Common materials:

1. **Aluminum**

   o **Pros**: Lightweight, strong, easy to machine or cut.

   o **Cons**: Can be more expensive than acrylic or wood.

   o **Usage**: Frame of mid-sized or large robots.

2. **Acrylic or PVC**

   o **Pros**: Low cost, easy to laser cut.

   o **Cons**: Can crack under stress, less robust for heavier builds.

   o **Usage**: Small desktop or educational robots.

3. **Steel**

   o **Pros**: Very strong, can handle large loads.

   o **Cons**: Heavy, often overkill for small robots.

   o **Usage**: Industrial or heavy-duty mobile platforms.

4. **3D Printed Parts**

- o **Pros**: Rapid prototyping, custom shapes, internal geometry.

- o **Cons**: May not withstand high stress or temperature, depending on the filament.

- o **Usage**: Brackets, sensor mounts, custom housings.

Rhetorical Question: How much weight must your robot carry, and under what environmental conditions (outdoors vs. indoors)? The answers typically guide material selection.

6.2.2 Weight Distribution and Center of Gravity

A poorly balanced robot risks tipping over during acceleration or on ramps. Place heavy components (batteries, motors) as **low** and **centered** as possible:

- **Even Weight** over the drive wheels for maximum traction.

- **Caster Wheels**: If you use a 3- or 4-wheeled design with casters, ensure the center of gravity is close to the drive axle.

- **Mounting**: Keep the battery and heavier electronics in symmetrical positions to avoid listing to one side.

6.2.3 Shock Absorption and Durability

Vibration from motors or rough terrain can loosen screws or damage sensitive sensors. Options to mitigate:

1. **Rubber Dampers** between motors and chassis.

2. **Lock Washers or Thread-Locking Compound** (like Loctite) on fasteners.

3. **Shock-Absorbing Mounts** for electronics or LIDAR units that need stable alignment.

6.2.4 Diagram 2: Basic Robot Chassis Layout

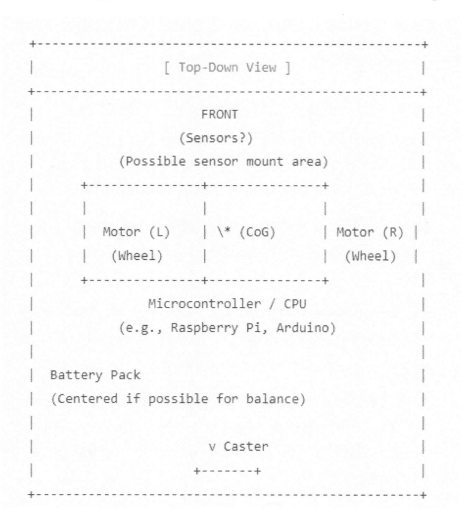

```
+--------------------------------------------------+
|                [ Top-Down View ]                 |
+--------------------------------------------------+
|                    FRONT                         |
|                  (Sensors?)                      |
|            (Possible sensor mount area)          |
|      +---------------+---------------+           |
|      |               |               |           |
|      | Motor (L)     | \* (CoG)      | Motor (R) |
|      | (Wheel)       |               | (Wheel)   |
|      +---------------+---------------+           |
|              Microcontroller / CPU               |
|            (e.g., Raspberry Pi, Arduino)         |
|                                                  |
| Battery Pack                                     |
| (Centered if possible for balance)               |
|                                                  |
|                  v Caster                        |
|                +-------+                         |
+--------------------------------------------------+
```

6.3 Wiring and Hardware Setup for ROS2 Compatibility

Hardware assembly is more than just screwing parts together. You must also ensure the electronics can be recognized and controlled by **ROS2** nodes running on your chosen computing platform.

6.3.1 Choosing a Single-Board Computer or Microcontroller

You need some form of **computing unit** to run ROS2:

- **Raspberry Pi 4** or **NVIDIA Jetson Nano**: Common choices for moderate computing tasks, including sensor fusion and some vision processing.

- **Intel NUC**: More powerful, suitable for heavy computations like advanced SLAM or neural networks.

- **Microcontroller boards** (like an Arduino) can handle real-time motor control, but usually you offload ROS2 to a more capable companion computer.

- **ROS2 on Microcontrollers** (Micro-ROS) is emerging, but it's still specialized—most users still rely on a Pi or similar SBC (Single Board Computer) for the main ROS2 brain.

Pro Tip: *If you're only controlling a couple of DC motors and reading simple sensors, a Pi 4 is often enough. If you want advanced computer vision at real-time speeds, consider a Jetson or an Intel-based system with GPU acceleration.*

6.3.2 Communication Interfaces

Hardware interfaces must tie your motors, drivers, and sensors back to your SBC:

1. **GPIO Pins**: General-purpose I/O for digital signals like direction or step pulses.

2. **UART/Serial**: Simple, point-to-point communication with motor drivers or sensor modules.

3. **I2C or SPI**: Common for IMUs, some range sensors, or LCD displays.

4. **USB**: Many cameras, LIDARs, or plug-and-play sensor modules rely on USB.

5. **Ethernet or Wi-Fi**: Vital if you want wireless telemetry, remote control, or multi-robot coordination.

6.3.3 Power Wiring Basics

Organize power wiring so motors (high current lines) are separate from sensitive signals:

1. **Thicker Wires** for motor supply to handle high current draw.

2. **Fuses or Resettable Breakers** on battery leads to prevent damage if a short occurs.

3. **Distribution Board** or terminal blocks to route power to motor drivers, regulators, and logic boards.

Step-by-Step:

1. **Mount** your battery in the chassis.

2. **Connect** battery leads to a main power switch or fuse.

3. **Distribute** power through an appropriate gauge wire to each motor driver.

4. **Run** a separate line from the battery (or from a buck converter) to the SBC's power input (e.g., 5 V regulator for a Raspberry Pi).

6.3.4 ROS2 Integration

Once you have an SBC with ROS2 installed:

- **Motor Control Node:** Possibly a Python or C++ node that sends PWM commands or velocity topics to a microcontroller, which in turn drives the motors.

- **Sensor Nodes:** The device drivers (some are built into ROS2 packages) that publish sensor data on relevant topics.

- **Topic Names:** E.g., /cmd_vel for velocity commands, /odom for odometry data, and so on.

- **Launch Files:** Automate starting all relevant nodes at once.

Key: Make sure your hardware is recognized by the OS. For instance, a USB LIDAR might appear as /dev/ttyUSB0, or a *camera as /dev/video0. In your launch file, reference these device paths or use **udev rules** to create stable names (e.g., /dev/lidar).*

6.4 Integrating Sensors (LIDAR, Ultrasonic, Camera) on a Physical Robot

Now that the foundation is set—motors, power, computing platform—we can **mount and connect** sensors. The real world is rarely as predictable as a simulator, so robust sensor data is crucial for mapping, obstacle avoidance, and autonomous decision-making.

6.4.1 LIDAR Setup

1. **Mounting Height:** Usually near the robot's top or front, so the beam sweeps a clear 2D plane.

2. **Vibration Isolation:** LIDAR accuracy can degrade if it vibrates excessively. A small foam or rubber mount can help.

3. **Connecting:** If your LIDAR uses USB or serial, route cables carefully away from motor power lines to reduce electrical noise.

4. **Calibration:** Many LIDARs have minimal calibration, but check if your device requires steps like setting the rotational offset or verifying range accuracy.

6.4.2 Ultrasonic Sensors

Ultrasonic "pings" can detect close-range obstacles, especially in blind spots that LIDAR might miss. Consider:

- **Placement:** Often mounted in multiple directions around the robot's perimeter.

- **Data Fusion:** Combine with LIDAR data for improved near-field obstacle sensing.

- **Interference:** If using multiple ultrasonic sensors simultaneously, they can produce overlapping echoes. Stagger triggers or operate them one at a time if crosstalk is an issue.

6.4.3 Cameras

- **Mount** a camera at an angle that covers the robot's forward path. For overhead tasks, mount upward or use a tilt mechanism.

- **Lighting Conditions:** If operating in low light, consider IR or depth sensors (e.g., RealSense).

- **Focus** on stable mounting—cameras with large vibrations can cause motion blur.

- **ROS2 Node:** A typical camera node might publish /camera/image_raw; calibration using tools like camera_calibration is recommended for accurate measurements.

Rhetorical Question: Could your robot rely on LIDAR alone, or would a camera provide richer data for tasks like object recognition?

6.4.4 Combining Sensor Outputs

In advanced builds, you might have multiple sensors running concurrently:

- **Sensor Fusion** frameworks or ROS2 packages help create a unified data stream.

- **tf2** transforms define each sensor's position relative to the robot's base.

- **Launch Files** bring up each sensor driver node, set parameters for data rates, and create a complete system for environment perception.

6.5 Hands-On: Assembling a Small Autonomous Mobile Robot

We've covered the theory—now let's put it into practice with a detailed, **step-by-step** guide to building a **small, autonomous mobile robot**. Our example robot will use:

- Two DC brushed motors (with built-in gearboxes).

- A Raspberry Pi 4 as the main computing unit.

- A 2D LIDAR for navigation.

- A small battery pack (LiPo or NiMH).

- An H-bridge motor driver (like a TB6612 or L298N).

- Optional ultrasonic or camera sensors for extra perception.

Note: The exact parts are flexible. Feel free to substitute based on availability and budget.

6.5.1 Materials and Tools

1. **Chassis Kit:** A ready-made metal or acrylic base with cutouts for motors and wheels.

2. **DC Motors:** Gearbox motors rated around 6–12 V, 100–300 RPM.

3. **Motor Driver:** TB6612-based board or L298N module.

4. **Battery:** LiPo 2S (~7.4 V) or NiMH 6–9 V pack.

5. **Voltage Regulator:** 5 V buck converter for the Pi.

6. **Raspberry Pi 4** (4 GB RAM recommended).

7. **MicroSD Card:** At least 16 GB, loaded with a ROS2-compatible OS (e.g., Ubuntu 20.04 + ROS2 Foxy).

8. **LIDAR Sensor:** e.g., RPLIDAR A1 or YDLIDAR X4 (USB or serial).

9. **Cables, Connectors, Screws**, and mechanical hardware.

10. **Basic Tools:** Screwdrivers, wire strippers, soldering iron (optional), hex keys, zip ties.

6.5.2 Step 1: Physical Assembly of the Chassis

1. **Unbox** your chassis kit. Identify top plate, bottom plate, motor mounting brackets, wheels, and caster (if included).

2. **Attach** the motors to their brackets. Make sure they're secure and aligned with the chassis holes.

3. **Install** the wheels onto the motor shafts, verifying they spin freely.

4. **Mount** the caster wheel or rear support.

5. **Confirm** the robot can roll on a flat surface without wobbling.

6.5.3 Step 2: Mounting Electronics and Battery

1. **Place** the motor driver board in a safe spot, typically near the motors to minimize wire length.

2. **Secure** the Raspberry Pi. Some chassis kits include standoffs for SBCs. If not, drill small holes or use adhesive standoffs.

3. **Locate** the battery in a central area to balance weight. Use Velcro straps or a battery tray to keep it firmly in place.

4. **Plan** wire routes so that you can keep data lines away from high-current motor wires if possible.

Diagram 3 : *Wiring Layout for a Simple Two-Wheeled Robot*

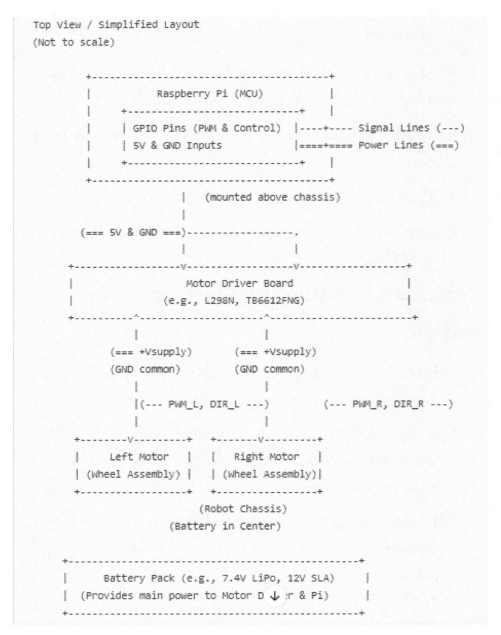

```
Top View / Simplified Layout
(Not to scale)


        +------------------------------------------+
        |              Raspberry Pi (MCU)          |
        |   +----------------------------+    |
        |   | GPIO Pins (PWM & Control)  |----+---- Signal Lines (---)
        |   | 5V & GND Inputs            |====+==== Power Lines (===)
        |   +----------------------------+    |
        +------------------------------------------+
                  |   (mounted above chassis)
                  |
     (=== 5V & GND ===)------------------.
                  |                   |
        +-----------------v----------------v-----------------+
        |               Motor Driver Board               |
        |            (e.g., L298N, TB6612FNG)             |
        +--------------^-------------------^-----------------+
                  |                   |
             (=== +Vsupply)       (=== +Vsupply)
             (GND common)         (GND common)
                  |                   |
             |(--- PWM_L, DIR_L ---)          (--- PWM_R, DIR_R ---)
                  |                   |
        +--------v---------+   +-------v---------+
        |   Left Motor   |   |  Right Motor  |
        | (Wheel Assembly) |   | (Wheel Assembly)|
        +------------------+   +-----------------+
                  (Robot Chassis)
                  (Battery in Center)


        +---------------------------------------------+
        |    Battery Pack (e.g., 7.4V LiPo, 12V SLA)  |
        |  (Provides main power to Motor D ↓ :r & Pi) |
        +---------------------------------------------+
```

Notes:

1. Battery Pack powers both the Motor Driver and the Raspberry Pi.

 - The Motor Driver typically needs a higher voltage (e.g., 6–12V) for motors.

 - A regulator or DC-DC converter may supply **5V** to the Pi.

2. Raspberry Pi

 - Receives **5V and GND** from the battery (through a regulator).

 - Outputs **PWM** and **Direction** signals to the Motor Driver via GPIO pins.

3. Motor Driver Board

 - Provides H-Bridge functionality to drive both motors.

 - Takes the PWM/Direction signals from the Pi and the motor power from the battery.

 - Outputs appropriate voltage/current to each motor.

4. Motors (Left and Right)

 - Each connected to its own driver channel.

- Receive variable voltage (based on PWM) for speed control and direction changes.

5. Common Ground

- The Raspberry Pi and Motor Driver must share a ground reference.

Arrows and lines indicate the **flow of power** (bold `` `===` ``) and **control signals** (dashed `` `---` ``). This layout ensures clear separation of power and signal wiring, helping reduce noise and simplify troubleshooting.

6.5.4 Step 3: Wiring and Connectivity

1. **Motor Driver to Motors**: Two wires per motor channel (motor A, motor B). Ensure correct polarity for forward rotation.

2. **Motor Driver to Battery:** Provide the driver's VM input with battery voltage (7.4 V from a 2S LiPo, for instance).

3. **Motor Driver to Raspberry Pi:** Connect **PWM** (e.g., GPIO pins 12 and 13) and **direction pins** (GPIO pins 5 and 6). Also provide ground reference between Pi and driver.

4. **Voltage Regulator:** Tap the battery's output to a buck converter set to 5 V, feeding the Pi's 5 V and ground pins.

5. **LIDAR**: If it's USB, simply connect to the Pi's USB port. If serial, wire TX/RX lines to Pi's UART pins (while crossing TX->RX, RX->TX).

6. **Optional Sensors**: E.g., ultrasonic modules on GPIO pins (trigger/echo). Keep them separate from the motor lines to reduce noise.

6.5.5 Step 4: ROS2 Setup on the Raspberry Pi

1. **Install Ubuntu 20.04** on the Pi.

2. **Install ROS2** (e.g., Foxy or Galactic). Follow official instructions to add the ROS2 repository and run apt-get install.

3. **Configure** your workspace (e.g., ~/ros2_ws) for any custom packages like a motor control node or sensor drivers.

4. **Enable I2C, SPI, or UART** (if needed) via raspi-config or the appropriate system tool.

5. **Create** a launch file that starts your motor control node, LIDAR driver, and sensor nodes at boot. For instance:

```bash
```

```
ros2 launch my_robot_bringup bringup.launch.py
```

6.5.6 Step 5: Motor Control Node and Odometry

Motor Control Node (example in Python): Subscribes to /cmd_vel and translates linear/angular velocity commands into PWM signals for the motor driver. For differential drive:

- Let /cmd_vel contain **linear.x** for forward speed, **angular.z** for turning.

- Convert these speeds to left/right wheel velocities.

- Apply a **PID** loop to maintain the requested velocity, using wheel encoders if available.

- Publish /odom messages with the robot's estimated position and orientation over time.

Tip: If your motors lack encoders, you won't have accurate odometry. Consider adding magnetic or optical encoders to the motor shafts for closed-loop control.

6.5.7 Step 6: LIDAR Node and Basic Obstacle Avoidance

Install your LIDAR's ROS2 driver package (e.g., rplidar_ros2) or use any official driver from the vendor. This node will publish LaserScan messages on, say, /scan. You can do a **basic test:**

1. **Run** the LIDAR node:

```bash
bash
```

```
ros2 run rplidar_ros rplidar_node
```

2. **Open** RViz:

```bash
bash
```

```
rviz2
```

3. **Add** a LaserScan display. Set topic to /scan. Confirm you see distance data rotating in a circular pattern.

Obstacle Avoidance: If you want rudimentary collision prevention, you can create a node that monitors LaserScan data and stops or slows the robot when an obstacle is detected within a certain range. More advanced solutions integrate with the ROS2 Navigation stack (nav2) for mapping and path planning.

6.5.8 Step 7: Testing and Calibration

1. **Ground Test:** Elevate the robot so wheels can spin freely. Send small velocity commands:

```bash
bash
```

```
ros2 topic pub /cmd_vel geometry_msgs/msg/Twist
"{linear: {x: 0.1}, angular: {z: 0.0}}"
```

Check if wheels spin forward. Reverse the polarity if needed.

2. **Drive Test:** Place the robot on the floor, gradually increase speed. Verify no wiring tangles or mechanical friction.

3. **Adjust Gains**: If using a PID for velocity control, start with small P, I, D values and slowly increase until the robot moves smoothly without oscillations or lag.

6.5.9 Step 8: Expanding Capabilities

Once you have a baseline working:

- **Navigation Stack**: Add a map server and local planner for advanced autonomy.

- **Additional Sensors**: Attach an IMU, camera, or ultrasonic ring for 360° coverage.

- **Battery Monitoring**: Use an ADC or specialized sensor to read battery voltage, then publish a ROS2 topic for battery level warnings.

- **Remote Teleoperation**: Launch a joystick or keyboard teleop node to override autonomous behavior when needed.

Chapter Summary

Congratulations—you've journeyed through the essential steps of **Real-World Robot Building and Integration**. Let's recap the key points:

1. **Choosing Motors, Motor Drivers, and Power Systems**

    ◦ **DC, Stepper,** or **Brushless** motors each suit different performance needs.

- o **Drivers** like H-bridges or ESCs turn control signals into powerful outputs.

- o **Power** must be stable, with appropriate **batteries** and **voltage regulation** for both motors and electronics.

2. Mechanical Design Considerations

- o Material selection—aluminum, acrylic, steel, or 3D prints—depends on budget and load capacity.

- o Weight distribution and shock absorption matter for stable operation.

- o Keep the center of gravity low and balanced.

3. Wiring and Hardware Setup for ROS2

- o Select a **Single-Board Computer** or microcontroller for your computational needs.

- o Organize power and signals—thick wires for motors, shielded or separate lines for sensitive sensors.

- o Use recognized device names in your **ROS2** nodes or launch files.

4. Integrating Sensors (LIDAR, Ultrasonic, Camera)

- o Mount them securely, ensuring minimal vibration and suitable fields of view.

- ○ Combine sensor outputs with a **sensor fusion** strategy if needed.

- ○ Pay attention to wiring distances and potential interference.

5. **Hands-On: Assembling a Small Autonomous Mobile Robot**

- ○ A practical, step-by-step approach: mount chassis, install motors, add electronics, wire up power and signals, test using a **ROS2** environment.

- ○ Use a **motor control node** to handle velocity commands, a **LIDAR node** for obstacle detection, and optionally expand with a camera or ultrasonic sensors.

- ○ Tweak PID gains, calibrate sensors, and follow best practices for robust wiring.

*No Repetition: This chapter stands on its own, focusing specifically on **physical construction and integration** without rehashing earlier material on software or simulation.*

Where to Go from Here?

1. **Advanced Hardware:** Experiment with brushless motors, advanced suspensions, or specialized sensor arrays.

2. **Industrial-Grade Designs**: Explore metal frames, IP67-rated components for harsh environments, or redundant power systems.

3. **Large-Scale Power:** Investigate higher-voltage batteries, advanced battery management systems, or regenerative braking for bigger robots.

4. **Manufacturing and Enclosure**: Delve into professional methods like CNC machining, injection molding, or welded frames for robust designs.

5. **Full Autonomy:** Integrate the **ROS2 Navigation Stack** or custom planning algorithms for dynamic, multi-sensor autonomy.

With this knowledge in hand, you're ready to physically realize your robotic dreams—transitioning from conceptual or simulated designs into **tangible, working machines**. The **hands-on** experience is both exciting and enlightening, as you'll discover how intricacies in hardware can shape software decisions, and vice versa. Embrace the iterative process of testing, refining, and upgrading; it's all part of building real-world robots that can see, move, and interact with their surroundings.

Chapter 7: Advanced Topics in Autonomous Systems

Autonomous robotics has evolved far beyond single robots performing isolated tasks. Modern systems involve **fleets** of robots collaborating in dynamic environments, harnessing **machine learning** for perception, leveraging **edge computing** for real-time processing, and connecting to the **cloud** for fleet-wide coordination. Understanding these advanced topics is key to scaling robotic applications from small prototypes to enterprise-level deployments.

In this chapter, we'll explore:

1. **Multi-Robot Communication** (coordinating multiple units in real time).

2. **Fleet Management** (logistics and scheduling in industries like warehousing).

3. **Machine Learning and Computer Vision** (enabling high-level perception).

4. **Edge Computing and Cloud Integration** (balancing local vs. remote processing).

5. **Hands-On**: Building a **simple object detection** pipeline using Python, giving a taste of how robots can

recognize and respond to their surroundings in real time.

7.1 Multi-Robot Communication and Coordination

7.1.1 The Rationale for Multi-Robot Systems

Why involve multiple robots? In many real-world scenarios—such as warehouse picking, search-and-rescue missions, or agricultural field coverage—**one robot** can only do so much. A **multi-robot** approach allows parallel operation: one can transport items while another scans inventory or updates a digital map. Collaboration increases efficiency and coverage, especially when tasks can be split into smaller sub-tasks.

Rhetorical Question: Have you ever watched a colony of ants work together, each performing a small role that adds up to a massive collective result? That's the essence of multi-robot coordination.

7.1.2 Communication Infrastructures

For robots to coordinate, they must exchange data (sensor readings, task statuses, location updates). Common communication methods include:

1. **Wi-Fi or Ethernet**: Straightforward for indoor settings with existing network infrastructures.

2. **Mesh Networks**: Each robot acts as a node in a dynamic network. If one link fails, data can reroute via others.

3. **5G or Cellular**: Useful for wide-area deployments or outdoor scenarios.

4. **ROS2**: Provides a built-in discovery mechanism and messaging system, but multi-robot deployments can require careful configuration of domain IDs and network settings.

Latency and Bandwidth Concerns

- **High Bandwidth** tasks (streaming camera feeds from multiple robots) may overwhelm standard Wi-Fi.

- **Latency** is critical in real-time coordination—if a robot only receives updates with significant delay, collisions or suboptimal actions might occur.

7.1.3 Coordination Strategies

1. **Centralized Coordination**: One "master node" or server keeps track of all robots, assigning tasks and routes.

2. **Decentralized Coordination**: Robots negotiate among themselves, distributing tasks or forming sub-teams dynamically. This approach is more robust to single-point failures.

3. **Hybrid**: Centralized scheduling but local, decentralized collision avoidance.

Analogy: *Think of centralized coordination as an orchestra with a single conductor. Decentralized coordination is a jazz ensemble improvising in real time, each musician listening to the others.*

7.1.4 Diagram 1: Multi-Robot Communication Framework

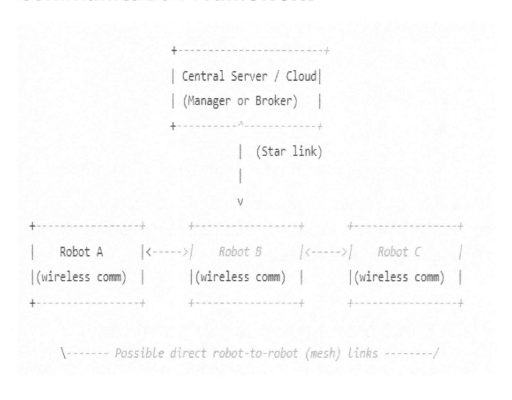

7.2 Fleet Management in Warehouses and Industrial Settings

7.2.1 The Rise of Robotic Fleets

Modern warehouses frequently employ **fleets of autonomous mobile robots (AMRs)** or **automated guided vehicles (AGVs)**. They can:

- Retrieve inventory racks,
- Handle pallet transport,
- Sort packages or supplies,
- Move goods between different stages of production.

Rhetorical Question: Can you imagine a distribution center processing tens of thousands of items a day without robots orchestrating the movement?

7.2.2 Fleet Management Components

A **fleet management system** typically handles:

1. **Task Allocation:** Distributing tasks (pick up item X, deliver it to station Y) among available robots.

2. **Resource Scheduling:** Managing charging stations, maintenance times, or specialized attachments needed for certain tasks.

3. **Traffic Control:** Ensuring robots don't collide or block each other in narrow aisles, possibly integrating digital "traffic lights" or "one-way lanes."

4. **Monitoring and Analytics:** Logging robot statuses, performance metrics, and overall throughput.

Diagram 2 :

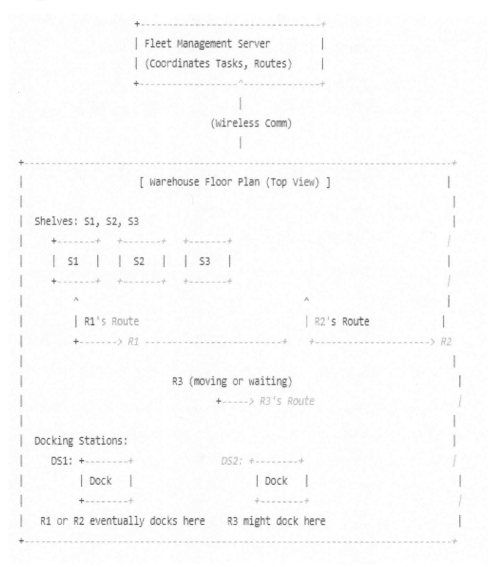

```
                +---------------------------------+
                | Fleet Management Server         |
                | (Coordinates Tasks, Routes)     |
                +------------------^--------------+
                                  |
                          (Wireless Comm)
                                  |
+-----------------------------------------------------------------+
|              [ Warehouse Floor Plan (Top View) ]                |
|                                                                 |
| Shelves: S1, S2, S3                                             |
|    +--------+   +--------+   +--------+                         |
|    |  S1  |   |  S2  |   |  S3  |                               |
|    +--------+   +--------+   +--------+                         |
|       ^                            ^                            |
|       | R1's Route               | R2's Route                  |
|    +-------> R1 ----------------------+   +---------------> R2  |
|                                                                 |
|                  R3 (moving or waiting)                         |
|                    +-----> R3's Route                           |
|                                                                 |
| Docking Stations:                                               |
|    DS1: +--------+          DS2: +--------+                     |
|         | Dock   |               | Dock   |                    |
|         +--------+               +--------+                    |
|   R1 or R2 eventually docks here   R3 might dock here           |
+-----------------------------------------------------------------+
```

7.2.3 Key Algorithms and Approaches

1. **Path Planning**: Often uses a **global map** of the warehouse with well-defined routes or graph-based navigation.

2. **Task Scheduling**: May rely on heuristics, such as the **Hungarian algorithm** for assignment problems, or more advanced methods like **Mixed Integer Linear Programming** for large-scale optimization.

3. **Queueing Models**: In complex environments, queueing theory helps handle arrival rates of tasks vs. capacity of robots.

7.2.4 Safety and Human-Robot Interaction

Many warehouses have **human workers** picking or supervising. Safety measures include:

- LIDAR-based detection to stop or slow when people approach.

- Visual/auditory alerts on robot movement.

- Clear demarcation of areas for robots vs. humans.

*Clarity: Standards like **ISO 3691-4** detail safety rules for driverless industrial trucks. In real implementations, compliance with such norms is crucial.*

7.3 Machine Learning and Computer Vision Applications

7.3.1 The Power of ML in Robotics

Robots once relied heavily on **handcrafted rules** (if distance < threshold, turn left). Today, **machine learning (ML)**, particularly **deep learning**, offers more powerful, adaptable perception and decision-making:

1. **Object Recognition:** Identifying boxes, people, or tools on a conveyor belt.

2. **Pose Estimation:** Estimating the orientation or position of objects or even human limbs.

3. **Navigation in Unstructured Environments:** Instead of purely geometric path planning, ML-based systems can learn which paths are safer or more efficient.

Rhetorical Question: *Isn't it amazing that a robot can "learn" to detect an object from thousands of examples, rather than you coding if-else statements for every shape variation?*

7.3.2 Convolutional Neural Networks (CNNs)

For **vision-based tasks**, **CNNs** remain the go-to architecture:

- **Feature Extraction:** Early layers act like filters, capturing edges, corners, or textures.

- **Classification or Segmentation:** Later layers piece together features to identify full objects or pixel-level classes.

- **Popular Models:** YOLO, Faster R-CNN, SSD, Mask R-CNN, etc.

7.3.3 Reinforcement Learning (RL)

RL trains an agent (robot) by rewarding certain actions in an environment. Over many trials, the robot "learns" policies that maximize cumulative reward (e.g., reaching a goal or avoiding collisions). This approach sees use in advanced navigation or manipulation tasks, though it can be data-intensive and require careful simulation or safe training environments.

7.3.4 Real-Time Constraints

Deploying ML on a robot requires real-time or near-real-time performance:

- **Accelerators:** GPUs, TPUs, or specialized deep learning chips.

- **Model Optimization:** Techniques like **quantization** or **pruning** can shrink models for faster inference with minimal accuracy loss.

- **Edge vs. Cloud:** Deciding which computations to run locally vs. uploading to a server for heavy processing (explored further in Section 7.4).

7.4 Edge Computing and Cloud Integration

7.4.1 Edge vs. Cloud: A Balancing Act

Edge computing means doing as much processing as possible directly on the robot (or a nearby gateway), reducing reliance on remote servers. **Cloud integration** harnesses massive compute resources and data storage, enabling advanced analytics or global fleet management.

Analogy: Edge computing is like cooking in your own kitchen for speed and convenience. Cloud integration is akin to sending tasks to a specialized chef who can handle large volumes but is located far away.

7.4.2 Why Edge Computing?

- **Latency:** Some decisions—like obstacle avoidance—need instantaneous response. Sending data to the cloud would be too slow.

- **Bandwidth:** Video streams or LIDAR data can consume large bandwidth, so local processing can be more efficient.

- **Reliability:** If the network fails, the robot can still operate autonomously with local compute resources.

7.4.3 Why Cloud Integration?

- **Global Coordination:** A central system can gather data from multiple robots, identify patterns, or optimize scheduling.

- **Big Data:** Machine learning model training often requires huge datasets. Doing it in the cloud is more practical than on a single SBC.

- **Scalability:** As your fleet grows, you can scale cloud instances rather than upgrading each robot's hardware.

7.4.4 Hybrid Architecture

Most advanced autonomous systems use a hybrid approach:

1. **Local Real-Time:** Edge computing handles immediate sensor fusion, control loops, or collision avoidance.

2. **Periodic Sync:** Robots periodically upload aggregated data to the cloud, where global algorithms refine planning or dispatch tasks.

3. **Model Updates:** The cloud can train improved ML models offline and push the new parameters back to robots at intervals.

Diagram 3 : *Edge-Cloud Hybrid Architecture*

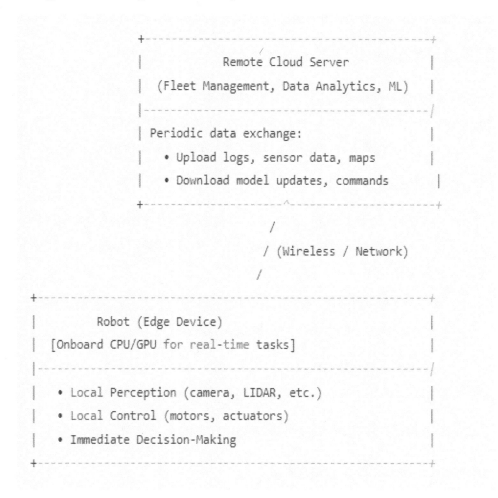

```
+------------------------------------------------+
|              Remote Cloud Server               |
|  (Fleet Management, Data Analytics, ML)        |
|------------------------------------------------/
| Periodic data exchange:                        |
|   • Upload logs, sensor data, maps             |
|   • Download model updates, commands           |
+----------------------^-------------------------+
                      /
                     / (Wireless / Network)
                    /
+------------------------------------------------+
|        Robot (Edge Device)                     |
|  [Onboard CPU/GPU for real-time tasks]         |
|------------------------------------------------/
|   • Local Perception (camera, LIDAR, etc.)     |
|   • Local Control (motors, actuators)          |
|   • Immediate Decision-Making                  |
+------------------------------------------------+
```

7.5 Hands-On: Implementing a Simple Object Detection Pipeline with Python

To conclude this chapter, let's **build a small machine learning pipeline** in Python to detect objects in images—a stepping stone toward real-time robotic perception. We'll keep it straightforward, focusing on essential steps so you can see how **computer vision** integrates into robotics.

7.5.1 Project Overview

Goal: Use a **pre-trained neural network** (like YOLO or a MobileNet-based classifier) to detect a few object classes (e.g., person, bottle, dog) in static images or a camera feed.

Prerequisites:

1. A **Python 3** environment with libraries like OpenCV, numpy, and a deep learning framework (e.g., torch or tensorflow).

2. Basic knowledge of Python scripts and environment management (pip, conda, etc.).

3. Ideally, a **webcam** or USB camera if you want real-time detection; otherwise, we'll use test images.

7.5.2 Step 1: Install Required Libraries

Assume a fresh environment:

```
pip install opencv-python numpy torch torchvision
```

(If you prefer TensorFlow, adjust accordingly.)

7.5.3 Step 2: Download a Pre-Trained Model

Let's pick a **MobileNet-based** object detection model available via **torchvision**:

```
python
```

```
import torch
import torchvision


# This is a pre-trained object detection model
from torchvision's model zoo
model =
torchvision.models.detection.fasterrcnn_resnet50_
fpn(pretrained=True)
model.eval()
```

Clarity: *This code snippet fetches a **Faster R-CNN** model with a **ResNet-50** backbone and a Feature Pyramid Network head. It's pre-trained on the **COCO dataset**, which includes 80 object classes.*

7.5.4 Step 3: Image Preprocessing

```python

import numpy as np
import cv2
from torchvision import transforms


# Define a transform that will resize and
normalize images for the model
transform = transforms.Compose([
    transforms.ToTensor(),  # converts to PyTorch
tensor, normalizing [0,1]
])
```

```python
def preprocess_image(image):
    # Convert from OpenCV BGR to RGB
    rgb_image = cv2.cvtColor(image,
cv2.COLOR_BGR2RGB)
    tensor_image = transform(rgb_image)
    return tensor_image
```

7.5.5 Step 4: Inference and Post-Processing

python

```python
def run_inference(model, image):
    # Preprocess
    input_tensor = preprocess_image(image)
    # Model expects a list of tensors
    with torch.no_grad():
        predictions = model([input_tensor])[0]  #
single image
    return predictions
```

The predictions dict typically contains:

- boxes: A list of bounding boxes ([x1, y1, x2, y2])
  around detected objects.

- labels: The predicted class IDs (like "person,"
  "bicycle," etc.).

- scores: Confidence scores from 0 to 1.

We can filter out low-confidence detections:

```python
def filter_predictions(predictions,
score_threshold=0.5):
    # Keep detections above a certain confidence
    keep_indices = [i for i, s in
enumerate(predictions['scores']) if s >
score_threshold]
    filtered_boxes =
predictions['boxes'][keep_indices]
    filtered_labels =
predictions['labels'][keep_indices]
    filtered_scores =
predictions['scores'][keep_indices]
    return filtered_boxes, filtered_labels,
filtered_scores
```

7.5.6 Step 5: Visualize Results

```python
COCO_INSTANCE_CATEGORY_NAMES = [
    '__background__', 'person', 'bicycle', 'car',
'motorcycle', 'airplane',
    # ... (list truncated for brevity) ...
    'toothbrush'
]
```

```python
def draw_detections(image, boxes, labels,
scores):
    for box, label, score in zip(boxes, labels,
scores):
        x1, y1, x2, y2 = map(int, box)
        cv2.rectangle(image, (x1, y1), (x2, y2),
(0, 255, 0), 2)
        caption =
f"{COCO_INSTANCE_CATEGORY_NAMES[label]}:
{score:.2f}"
        cv2.putText(image, caption, (x1, y1-10),
                cv2.FONT_HERSHEY_SIMPLEX,
0.5, (255, 0, 0), 2)
    return image
```

1. Draw a green rectangle around the bounding box.

2. Annotate the class name and confidence score.

7.5.7 Step 6: Putting It All Together

Combine everything into a single script object_detection.py:

```python
#!/usr/bin/env python3
import cv2
import torch
import torchvision
from torchvision import transforms
```

```python
# 1) Load the model
model =
torchvision.models.detection.fasterrcnn_resnet50_
fpn(pretrained=True)
model.eval()


# 2) Define a transform
transform = transforms.Compose([
    transforms.ToTensor()
])


# 3) Define helper functions
def preprocess_image(image):
    rgb_image = cv2.cvtColor(image,
cv2.COLOR_BGR2RGB)
    return transform(rgb_image)


COCO_INSTANCE_CATEGORY_NAMES = [ ... ]   # fill
the full list


def run_inference(model, image):
    input_tensor = preprocess_image(image)
    with torch.no_grad():
        predictions = model([input_tensor])[0]
    return predictions


def filter_predictions(predictions,
score_threshold=0.5):
```

```
    keep_indices = [i for i, s in
enumerate(predictions['scores']) if s >
score_threshold]
        boxes = predictions['boxes'][keep_indices]
        labels = predictions['labels'][keep_indices]
        scores = predictions['scores'][keep_indices]
        return boxes, labels, scores


def draw_detections(image, boxes, labels,
scores):
        for box, label, score in zip(boxes, labels,
scores):
            x1, y1, x2, y2 = map(int, box)
            cv2.rectangle(image, (x1, y1), (x2, y2),
(0, 255, 0), 2)
            caption =
f"{COCO_INSTANCE_CATEGORY_NAMES[label]}:
{score:.2f}"
            cv2.putText(image, caption, (x1, y1-10),
                    cv2.FONT_HERSHEY_SIMPLEX,
0.5, (255, 0, 0), 2)
        return image


if __name__ == "__main__":
    # 4) Capture from webcam or load an image
    cap = cv2.VideoCapture(0)  # 0 for default
webcam
    while True:
```

```
ret, frame = cap.read()
if not ret:
    break


predictions = run_inference(model, frame)
boxes, labels, scores =
filter_predictions(predictions, 0.5)
    output_frame = draw_detections(frame,
boxes, labels, scores)


    cv2.imshow("Object Detection",
output_frame)
    if cv2.waitKey(1) & 0xFF == ord('q'):
        break

cap.release()
cv2.destroyAllWindows()
```

7.5.8 Testing the Pipeline

1. **Connect** your webcam, ensure your system recognizes it.

2. **Run** python3 object_detection.py.

3. **Allow** a few seconds for the model to load.

4. **Observe** real-time bounding boxes and labels as you move objects in front of the camera.

5. **Experiment** with different score_threshold values to filter out uncertain detections.

Pro Tip: *If you want to deploy this on a robot, you can feed the camera frames from the robot's USB camera or even from a **ROS2 image topic** (using a Python node that subscribes to the camera feed, converts it to OpenCV format, and runs inference).*

7.5.9 Scaling to Real-Time Robotics

For a full **ROS2** integration:

- Create a **ROS2 node** that subscribes to /camera/image_raw.

- Convert sensor_msgs/Image to an OpenCV Mat.

- Run the detection pipeline, publish bounding boxes or recognized objects on a topic like /detected_objects.

- Optionally feed results into navigation or manipulation nodes that respond to these detections.

Hardware Acceleration:

- If you have a **Jetson** or **Intel GPU**, consider frameworks like **TensorRT** or **OpenVINO** to optimize inference.

- Tweak the model architecture to run at a higher FPS for real-time robot tasks.

Chapter Summary

In this **Advanced Topics** chapter, we've moved beyond single-robot fundamentals and delved into **multi-robot coordination, fleet management, machine learning, edge-cloud integration,** and even built a **simple computer vision pipeline:**

1. **Multi-Robot Communication and Coordination**

   o Explored centralized vs. decentralized approaches, highlighting Wi-Fi or mesh networks for distributed robot teams.

   o Emphasized the importance of robust communication to prevent collisions and maximize productivity.

2. **Fleet Management**

   o Showed how large groups of robots can streamline warehouse operations.

   o Covered path planning, task allocation, traffic control, and the significance of safety in human-robot environments.

3. **Machine Learning and Computer Vision**

   o Discussed deep learning's role in perception for complex tasks like object recognition, pose estimation, and learned navigation.

o Addressed the challenge of real-time inference and model optimization.

4. **Edge Computing and Cloud Integration**

o Examined how local (on-robot) processing can reduce latency and bandwidth usage.

o Showed that the cloud remains vital for global fleet coordination, model training, and large-scale data management.

5. **Hands-On: Simple Object Detection**

o Demonstrated a step-by-step approach to building a Python pipeline using **PyTorch** and **OpenCV**.

o Encouraged real-time testing with a webcam, bridging the gap between theory and practical deployment.

*No Repetition: This chapter presented **unique** advanced-level topics without rehashing earlier chapters' details on basic navigation or sensor integration.*

Where to Go Next?

1. **Advanced Multi-Robot SLAM**: Explore collaborative mapping, where multiple robots share partial maps.

2. **Reinforcement Learning**: Apply RL to real robots, learning advanced behaviors in navigation or manipulation.

3. **Cloud-Based Simulation**: Tools like **AWS RoboMaker** or **Gazebo** in the cloud allow large-scale testing of new software before deploying to real fleets.

4. **Edge AI Hardware**: Investigate specialized hardware like the **NVIDIA Jetson AGX** or **Coral Edge TPU** for better inference speeds.

5. **Ethical and Regulatory Aspects**: As robotics grows, so do concerns about data privacy, job displacement, and safety certifications.

By mastering multi-robot systems, ML-driven perception, and edge-cloud architectures, you can design **scalable, intelligent robotics solutions**. Each piece—communication, scheduling, real-time inference, global analytics—fits together to create an ecosystem far more powerful than any single-robot approach. The future of autonomy lies in networks of robots collaborating across factories, highways, fields, and homes—constantly learning, adapting, and growing to meet humanity's ever-evolving needs.

Chapter 8: Building Robots for Space Exploration — Advanced Robotic Systems

Robotics has found some of its most dramatic applications in **space exploration**. From the early days of the Soviet Lunokhod rovers on the Moon to NASA's sophisticated Perseverance rover on Mars, robots have allowed humanity to observe alien worlds without putting astronauts at immediate risk. But **space robotics** goes well beyond rovers—there are orbital servicing robots, robotic arms on space stations, and conceptual swarm systems for asteroid mining. Each scenario demands robust designs to handle extreme conditions, high latency communications, and reliability on cosmic timelines.

This chapter dives deep into **space robotics**, covering:

1. **Unique challenges** like temperature extremes, vacuum conditions, and communication delays.

2. **Advanced navigation** strategies blending classical approaches with AI-based methods.

3. **Teleoperation vs. Full Autonomy** considerations, especially given the vast distances involved.

4. **Future trends**—swarm robotics, in-situ resource utilization, and more.

5. **Hands-On**: How to **simulate a Mars-style rover mission** in a ROS2 environment, letting you experiment with interplanetary robotics from your home lab.

8.1 Unique Challenges in Space Robotics (Extreme Environments, Latency, Reliability)

8.1.1 Extreme Environments: Harsh Conditions Beyond Earth

Space is **unforgiving**. Robots operating on the Moon, Mars, or other celestial bodies face challenges rarely encountered on Earth:

1. **Temperature Fluctuations**: A single Martian day (sol) can see extreme temperature swings from -130°C at night to near 0°C in sunlight. Electronic components must be insulated or designed to work under these swings.

2. **Vacuum or Thin Atmosphere**: On the Moon, there's virtually no atmosphere to conduct heat away or provide aerodynamic braking. Mars has a thin CO_2 atmosphere (~1% of Earth's pressure). This affects cooling, sensor design, and mechanical mechanisms that rely on air.

3. **Radiation:** Solar and cosmic rays can damage electronics, causing bit flips or degradation over time. **Radiation-hardened** components or shielding is often mandatory.

4. **Dust and Regolith:** Fine Martian dust or lunar regolith is abrasive and sticky, jamming joints or clogging instruments.

Rhetorical Question: If common issues like dirt or heat can overwhelm Earth-bound robots, how much more demanding are sub-zero, radiation-soaked deserts with no quick rescue in sight?

8.1.2 High Communication Latency

Distance brings **delay.** For instance, radio signals to Mars can take anywhere from 4 to 24 minutes (round trip up to 48 minutes). This latency means real-time teleoperation is **impossible**—rover commands can take half an hour just to reach the robot, and confirmations take just as long to return.

- **Implication:** Missions must rely heavily on **preprogrammed autonomy** or short command sequences executed by the rover.

- **Store-and-Forward** Communication: The rover stores telemetry and sends data during scheduled windows when Earth's antennas can receive.

8.1.3 Reliability and Redundancy

Launching a space robot is expensive and offers **no easy repairs**. If a critical component fails, the mission could be over. Redundancy is key:

1. **Dual or Triple Systems**: Duplicate controllers, multiple power lines, or redundant communication paths.

2. **Failover Mechanisms**: If the primary system malfunctions, the backup takes over automatically.

3. **Radiation-Hardened Electronics**: Helps avoid single-event upsets (SEUs) caused by cosmic rays flipping bits in memory.

8.1.4 Diagram 1: Space Robot Environment Challenges

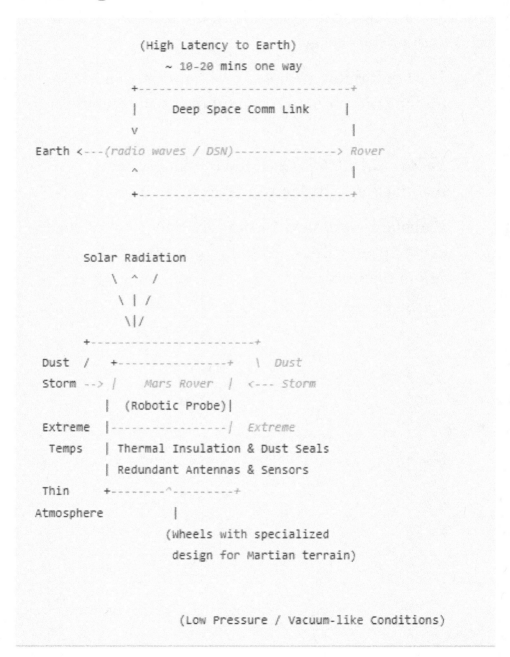

```
              (High Latency to Earth)
                 ~ 10-20 mins one way
           +---------------------------------+
           |        Deep Space Comm Link     |
           v                                 |
   Earth <---(radio waves / DSN)---------------> Rover
              ^                               |
           +---------------------------------+



          Solar Radiation
              \ ^ /
               \ | /
               \|/
            +-------------------------+
    Dust  /  +----------------+  \ Dust
    Storm --> |   Mars Rover   | <--- Storm
           | (Robotic Probe)|
    Extreme |-----------------|  Extreme
     Temps  | Thermal Insulation & Dust Seals
            | Redundant Antennas & Sensors
    Thin    +---------^---------+
  Atmosphere          |
                   (Wheels with specialized
                    design for Martian terrain)



                 (Low Pressure / Vacuum-like Conditions)
```

8.2 Advanced Navigation: Combining Traditional and AI-Based Approaches

8.2.1 Classical Robotics Navigation

Space agency rovers traditionally use **classical approaches** for navigation:

1. **Dead Reckoning:** Counting wheel rotations to estimate distance traveled. Prone to slip in loose regolith.

2. **Visual Odometry:** Stereo cameras track feature movement between images to compute relative motion. More accurate but computationally demanding.

3. **Feature-Based SLAM:** Landmarks in camera or LIDAR data anchor the rover's map. Usually, these algorithms run slowly to conserve power and ensure reliability.

Note: On Mars, GPS-style navigation is not available. Some missions rely on orbiters for approximate location referencing.

8.2.2 AI-Driven Navigation

With improved onboard computing, **machine learning** is increasingly used for:

1. **Terrain Classification:** Neural networks can label sand, rock, or bedrock, selecting safer or more interesting paths.

2. **Hazard Detection:** AI-based detection of large rocks, cliffs, or steep slopes from camera images.

3. **Adaptive Path Planning:** Reinforcement learning or advanced planners that adapt to changing terrain conditions.

Rhetorical Question: Why limit rovers to slow, cautious movement when AI might let them make faster decisions, exploring more terrain in the same mission time?

8.2.3 Hybrid Approaches

1. **Rule-Based Fallback:** Even if an AI model fails, the robot can default to simple obstacle detection with stereo vision.

2. **Limited Autonomy:** Mission controllers often require a path preview for critical movements, balancing AI's potential with human oversight.

3. **Onboard vs. Ground Processing:** Some rovers compress raw sensor data for Earth-based analysis, while advanced missions aim for real-time, onboard inference to reduce communication delays.

8.3 Teleoperation vs. Full Autonomy for Extraterrestrial Missions

8.3.1 Teleoperation: When Humans Pull the Strings

In short-latency scenarios—like operations on the International Space Station or near-lunar orbits—**teleoperation** can be viable:

- **Robotic Arms** on the ISS are often controlled by astronauts or ground operators in near-real time.

- **Low Earth Orbit** delay is negligible (1–2 seconds round trip).

- **Advantages**: Humans maintain direct oversight, enabling fine-grained manipulation tasks.

Analogy: Imagine remotely controlling a robot arm to fix a satellite's solar panel. If your latency is just a second or two, you can carefully align screws, much like a slow puzzle game.

8.3.2 Full Autonomy: Necessity for Deep Space

For **Mars rovers**, real-time teleoperation isn't feasible. Command sequences are usually uploaded daily, telling the rover where to drive and what experiments to perform. The rover must:

1. **Handle Obstacle Avoidance** on its own.

2. **Decide** if conditions (like wheel slip) are too risky.

3. **Report** data back to Earth for next day's plan.

Future missions to **outer planets** (e.g., Europa or Titan) will need even more autonomy, given communication lag could be hours.

8.3.3 Partial Autonomy: A Balanced Approach

Some tasks (like **sample collection**) might be partially teleoperated with advanced autonomy for hazard detection. Operators define high-level goals (e.g., "approach that rock outcrop, sample it"), and the robot orchestrates the how, stepping in only if new hazards or anomalies appear.

8.4 Future Trends: Swarm Robotics, In-Situ Resource Utilization, and More

8.4.1 Swarm Robotics

Instead of one large rover, imagine **dozens or hundreds** of small rovers working together:

1. **Scout Swarm**: Small scout bots map terrain quickly, searching for water ice or interesting geological features.

2. **Construction Swarm**: Multiple robots build habitats or infrastructure from local regolith.

3. **Communication Network**: Swarms can form ad hoc relay networks, ensuring coverage across wide areas.

Rhetorical Question: Why put all your eggs in one big, expensive rover when a swarm can provide redundancy and parallel tasks?

8.4.2 In-Situ Resource Utilization (ISRU)

Future exploration aims to **"live off the land"**:

- **Extracting water ice** from lunar or Martian soil.

- **Refining** local materials to produce oxygen or metals.

- **3D Printing** structures from regolith.

- Robots or robotic arms handle the excavation and processing. This reduces the mass of supplies transported from Earth.

8.4.3 Off-World Factories and Autonomous Mining

Robots could mine asteroids or the Moon for rare metals or helium-3:

1. **Low-Gravity Challenges**: In microgravity, a drilling arm can push a small craft away instead of penetrating the rock.

2. **Anchoring Mechanisms**: Grapples or harpoons fix the robot in place.

3. **Autonomous Processing:** Minimal human supervision means advanced autonomy for each mining step.

8.4.4 Diagram 2: Future Space Robotics Scenarios

```
+----------------------------------------------------+
|                  Panel 1: Mars Rover Swarm         |
|----------------------------------------------------/
|  Surface of Mars with multiple small rovers:       |
|      /R\           /R\            /R\               |
|     /   \         /   \          /   \             |
|    [ R1 ] ->    [ R2 ] ->     [ R3 ] ->            |
|     \   /         \   /          \   /             |
|      \R/           \R/            \R/              |
| (Swarm cooperation, solar panels on each rover,    |
|  shared comm links, coordinated exploration)       |
+----------------------------------------------------+


+----------------------------------------------------+
|          Panel 2: Lunar Habitat Construction       |
|----------------------------------------------------/
|  Robotic arms assembling structures on the Moon:|
|         [ Lunar Surface / Regolith ]              |
|             +-----------+                        /
| Bot A --->  | Habitat   |  <--- Bot B           /
|  (automated | Segment   | (holding beam)         |
|  crane)     +-----------+                       /
|       \                                    /  |
|        \------ > Next Habitat Section < -----/  |
| (Bots using specialized drills, regolith 3D-      |
|  printing, or crane arms; solar arrays for power)  |
+----------------------------------------------------+
```

```
+----------------------------------------------------+
|          Panel 3: Asteroid Mining & Extraction     |
|----------------------------------------------------/
|  A small mining bot tethered to a spinning rock:   |
|              Asteroid:    [ spinning ]             |
|                 /------------\                     /
|                /     (ore)     \                   |
|               (-----------------)  <- Bot's        /
|                \    tethered   /    anchor/tether  |
|                 \------------/                     /
|                      ^                             |
|         Robot with thrusters + sample extraction arm|
|         using solar panels for power & communications|
+----------------------------------------------------+
```

8.5 Hands-On: Simulating a Rover Mission in a Martian-Like ROS2 Environment

Now, let's get practical with a **simulation project** that mimics a Martian rover environment using ROS2. While you won't replicate the full complexity of NASA-grade rovers, this **hands-on** exercise introduces core concepts like terrain navigation, delayed command execution, and basic autonomy.

8.5.1 Project Overview

We'll use a **Gazebo** (or Ignition) simulation with:

1. A **Martian**-style terrain—reddish sand, some rock obstacles, maybe a crater.

2. A **rover** with six wheels (or four for simplicity), a camera, and a LIDAR.

3. **ROS2** nodes for environment mapping or navigation.

4. Optional **communication delay** simulation to mimic latency.

Step-by-Step: Building a simple mission script that drives the rover to a target rock, simulates sample collection, and returns data.

8.5.2 Step 1: Setting Up the Simulation World

1. **Install** Gazebo (or Ignition) for your ROS2 distribution.

2. **Download** or **create** a custom .sdf or .world file featuring a red desert with boulders. For realism, add:

php

```
<model name="martian_terrain">
  <!-- terrain mesh or heightmap -->
</model>
<model name="rock_obstacles">
```

<!-- random placement of rock models -->

</model>

3. **Include** a **sky** or environment plugin to mimic Martian lighting and colors. Some advanced mods can tweak gravity to 0.38g (Mars equivalent).

8.5.3 Step 2: Configuring the Rover

Let's assume a simplified 4-wheel rover:

1. **URDF** or **SDF** model specifying wheels, a **differential drive** or an **Ackermann steering** configuration.

2. **Sensors**:

    o **LIDAR** plugin publishing on /scan.

    o **Camera** plugin streaming an /image_raw topic.

    o **IMU** plugin on /imu.

3. **Power Source**: We'll keep it simple—no solar charging needed, just indefinite runtime in simulation.

4. **Mass**: Adjust to reflect a ~25–50 kg small rover if you're mimicking a smaller, experimental design.

Launch File snippet (conceptual):

```python
from launch import LaunchDescription
from launch.actions import
IncludeLaunchDescription
```

```
from launch.launch_description_sources import
PythonLaunchDescriptionSource
import os

def generate_launch_description():
    # Gazebo world file path
    world_file = os.path.join(

get_package_share_directory('my_martian_world'),
        'worlds',
        'martian_desert.world'
    )

    # Rover SDF or URDF file path
    rover_sdf = os.path.join(

get_package_share_directory('my_rover_description
'),
        'models',
        'rover.sdf'
    )

    return LaunchDescription([
        # Start Gazebo with Martian world
        IncludeLaunchDescription(
            PythonLaunchDescriptionSource([
                os.path.join(
```

```
get_package_share_directory('gazebo_ros'),
                'launch',
                'gazebo.launch.py')
        ]),
        launch_arguments={'world':
world_file}.items()
    ),
    # Spawn the rover
    Node(
        package='gazebo_ros',
        executable='spawn_entity.py',
        arguments=['-file', rover_sdf,
                '-entity',
'martian_rover',
                '-x', '0', '-y', '0', '-
z', '0.1'],
        output='screen'
    ),
])
```

8.5.4 Step 3: Basic Navigation and Autonomy

For a simple demonstration:

1. **Map Building** (Optional): Use **slam_toolbox** or a custom mapping node if you want the rover to construct a 2D map from LIDAR data.

2. **Local Planner**: A node that reads /scan and /odom, computing velocity commands to avoid boulders.

3. **Mission Script**: A Python node with a **state machine**:

   o **State 1**: Move forward until a certain distance from a rock.

   o **State 2**: Stop, simulate "sampling."

   o **State 3**: Return to the start or move to another waypoint.

Rhetorical Question: Isn't it more impressive if the rover can adapt to unexpected obstacles, rather than following a fixed path?

8.5.5 Step 4: Introducing Communication Delay (Optional)

To mimic **Mars-like latency**:

1. **ROS2** doesn't natively add artificial delay, but you can use third-party tools or a node that buffers messages for X seconds before relaying them.

2. **Algorithmic Approach**: If you want to replicate command up, telemetry down, run your mission script in a separate node that only forwards commands after a delay.

3. **Observing** the effect: You'll see the rover keep moving briefly after you send a stop command, emphasizing the importance of onboard autonomy.

8.5.6 Step 5: Testing Your Martian Rover

1. **Launch** the environment:

```
ros2 launch my_martian_world
martian_world.launch.py
```

2. **Check** that the rover spawns.

3. **Run** your mission script:

```
arduino
```

```
ros2 run my_rover_mission mission_node
```

4. **Monitor** in RViz:

   o Add /scan for LIDAR data.

   o Display /camera/image_raw for a first-person rover view.

   o Show TF frames (odom, base_link).

Diagram 3

```
+-------------------------------------------------------------------------+
|                    RViz: Mars Environment (Red Hue)                     |
+-------------------------------------------------------------------------+
| Displays (Left Panel):                                                  |
|   - RobotModel (Rover)                                                  |
|   - LaserScan (/scan)                                                   |
|   - TF (/tf)                                                            |
|   - Global/Local Costmaps                                               |
|   - Planned Path (/plan)                                                |
|   - Map or Occupancy Grid (/map) (if used)                              |
|                                                                         |
|                      Main Visualization Window                          |
|   +------------------------------------------------------------------+  |
|   |      [ (Red-Tinted) Simulated Martian Surface ]                  |  |
|   |                                                                  |  |
|   |                    [ Horizon in the Distance ] <----(red sky)    /  |
|   |                              ^                                   |  |
|   |           (Rock) O <-----+-----+                                 /  |
|   |    LIDAR Scan Arcs:       .   .  (obstacle)                      |  |
|   |      .            .   .     .                                    |  |
|   |         . .(Rover).     (Planned Path) >>>>>>>>>>>>               |  |
|   |           \__/  .                                                |  |
|   |           / \    .  .                                            |  |
|   |      <--- laser beams scanning --->                              /  |
|   |                                                                  |  |
|   +------------------------------------------------------------------+  |
|                                                                         |
| Status Bar / Console: "No Errors" - Visualizing in RViz...              |
+-------------------------------------------------------------------------+
```

8.5.7 Step 6: Extending the Simulation

- **Add** a manipulator arm to simulate sampling.

- **Incorporate** advanced path planning or reinforcement learning.

- **Compare** teleoperation modes (commands typed in with artificial delay) vs. local autonomy.

- **Integrate** multi-robot scenarios: Perhaps two rovers share a common map.

Congratulations! You've just scratched the surface of simulating space robotics in ROS2. Real missions demand meticulous testing, radiation-hardened hardware, and specialized communication protocols, but your simulated scenario demonstrates the **core concepts**.

Chapter Summary

This chapter on **Building Robots for Space Exploration** delves into the **unique challenges** and **advanced strategies** for robotic missions beyond Earth's cradle. Key points:

1. **Unique Challenges in Space Robotics**

   - **Harsh Environments**: Extreme temperatures, vacuum, dust, radiation.

   - **Long Latency**: Multi-minute communication delays to Mars or further.

   - **Reliability & Redundancy**: No easy repairs, so robust design and backup systems are essential.

2. **Advanced Navigation**

- o **Classical Methods**: Visual odometry, feature-based SLAM, limited computing budgets.

- o **AI Approaches**: Deep learning for terrain classification, hazard detection.

- o **Hybrid**: Combining cautious rule-based fallback with fast AI-based inference.

3. **Teleoperation vs. Full Autonomy**

- o **Teleoperation**: Suited for low Earth orbit or short-latency scenarios like the ISS.

- o **Full Autonomy**: Crucial on Mars or outer planets, given extreme delays.

- o **Partial Autonomy**: Balancing human oversight with onboard decision-making.

4. **Future Trends**

- o **Swarm Robotics**: Multiple small rovers or drones collaborating for exploration, construction, or resource gathering.

- o **In-Situ Resource Utilization**: Robots that harvest water or minerals from local terrain to reduce reliance on Earth supplies.

- o **Off-World Factories**: Mining asteroids or building lunar outposts with minimal human presence.

5. **Hands-On: Simulating a Rover Mission**

- o **Martian-Like World** in Gazebo.

- o **Rover Model** with wheels, camera, LIDAR.

- o **Mission Script** showing basic autonomy.

- o Optional **latency** to mimic distant communication constraints.

No Repetition: We focused on space robotics specifics—such as extreme environments, cosmic latency, and advanced future trends—without rehashing earlier chapters about hardware fundamentals or terrestrial navigation.

Where to Go Next?

1. **Detailed Environment Physics**: Simulate low gravity or partial gravity environments, including how rovers handle traction in dusty regolith.

2. **Radiation-Resistant Hardware**: Explore specialized microcontrollers, memory, or FPGAs used in actual deep-space craft.

3. **Autonomous Sample Return**: Investigate how NASA's Perseverance rover is preparing to store rock samples for future retrieval.

4. **Planetary Drones**: Look at **Ingenuity** (the Mars helicopter) for aerial exploration.

5. **Extreme Missions**: Missions to Venus, Titan, or Europa, each with drastically different conditions—

acidic atmospheres, cryogenic lakes, or subsurface oceans.

Space robotics pushes the boundaries of engineering and software design, reminding us that **autonomy** becomes even more vital when Earth's oversight can arrive minutes or hours too late. By combining classical robotics with AI and robust hardware design, humankind continues to expand its reach across the Solar System—and beyond.

Chapter 9: Troubleshooting, Testing, and Continuous Improvement

Building or **programming** a robot is never a "one-and-done" process. Real-world success hinges on a cycle of **troubleshooting** problems, **testing** solutions, and **continuously improving** the system. Whether you're fine-tuning a physical robot's behavior or iterating on advanced software algorithms, this chapter provides an **in-depth** look at the strategies, tools, and best practices you can use to ensure your ROS2-based robot remains **robust, performant,** and **well-documented.**

We'll start by examining common pitfalls in **ROS2** (and how to debug them), move on to testing methodologies (unit tests, integration tests, simulations), explore performance optimization for real-time or near real-time robotics, discuss how to document and share your projects effectively, and finish with a **hands-on** demonstration of a robust **testing pipeline** using ROS2 tools.

9.1 Common Issues and Debugging Techniques in ROS2

9.1.1 Why Debugging Matters

A single overlooked bug can cause your robot to spin in circles or fail dangerously in the presence of obstacles. The **distributed** nature of ROS2—where multiple nodes communicate over a network—can make diagnosing issues more complex than in traditional monolithic applications. However, once you develop an organized approach to **identify, isolate, and resolve** errors, you'll minimize downtime and keep your robotics project on track.

Rhetorical Question: Have you ever tried to follow a conversation in a crowded room, only to realize that one participant spoke a different language? That's sometimes how debugging ROS2 can feel: multiple nodes "talking" on different topics and a flurry of data that needs to be sorted out.

9.1.2 Common ROS2 Pitfalls

1. **Wrong Topic Names or Typos**

   o ROS2 nodes rely on precise topic names (e.g., /scan vs. /lidar_scan). A small typo in your code or launch file can result in no data flow.

- o **Solution:** Tools like ros2 topic list or ros2 topic info /topic_name help confirm if a node is publishing or subscribing to the correct name.

2. **Mismatched Message Types**

- o If your subscriber expects sensor_msgs/msg/LaserScan but the publisher sends std_msgs/msg/Float32, they can't communicate.

- o **Solution:** Double-check that both ends use the same message type. You can also run ros2 interface show sensor_msgs/msg/LaserScan to see the structure.

3. **Parameter and Launch File Confusion**

- o Some ROS2 nodes rely on YAML config files or command-line parameters. If you fail to pass the correct parameters, the node might crash or behave incorrectly.

- o **Solution:** Log statements to verify the loaded parameters. Tools like ros2 param list can confirm active parameters.

4. **QoS Incompatibilities**

- o Quality of Service profiles in ROS2 determine how data is transmitted. A best-effort publisher can't always communicate reliably with a subscriber requiring reliability.

- o **Solution:** Configure matching QoS settings. For example, set both publisher and subscriber to "reliable" or "best-effort."

5. **Network or Domain ID Issues**

   - o In multi-machine setups, each node must share the same ROS2 domain ID. Firewalls, VLANs, or different domain IDs can prevent node discovery.

   - o **Solution:** Check environment variables (like ROS_DOMAIN_ID), ensure your network is open to UDP broadcast, and that Fast DDS or other DDS backends are configured properly.

Analogy: Think of your system like a puzzle. Each node is a puzzle piece. They need the correct shape (message type), matching edges (QoS, domain ID), and correct position (topic name) to fit together seamlessly.

9.1.3 Debugging Techniques and Tools

1. **Print Statements and Logging**

   - o The simplest approach: RCLCPP_INFO() in C++ or self.get_logger().info() in Python to see what the node is doing.

   - o **Level:** Debug, Info, Warn, Error, or Fatal to categorize importance.

2. ROS2 CLI Commands

- o ros2 topic list: Lists all active topics.

- o ros2 topic echo /some_topic: Prints incoming messages to see what's being published.

- o ros2 node list: Shows which nodes are running.

- o ros2 service list: Reveals active services.

3. RQT and RViz Tools

- o **rqt_graph:** Visualizes the network of nodes and topics—great for spotting if something isn't connected.

- o **RViz:** Visualizes sensor data (LaserScan, images, point clouds). If data doesn't appear, you know your pipeline is broken.

4. ros2 doctor (where available)

- o Some ROS2 distributions include a "doctor" command that checks environment consistency, network settings, etc.

5. Breakdown Approach

- o **Isolate:** Temporarily remove or disable certain nodes or features.

- o **Test:** Reintroduce them one at a time to see where the conflict or error emerges.

- o **Document:** Keep notes on each debugging step for future reference.

9.2 Testing Methodologies: Unit Tests, Integration Tests, and Simulations

9.2.1 Why Test?

Bugs are inevitable. Structured **testing** ensures you catch them early, preventing small errors from causing big headaches. In robotics, testing becomes even more critical because code can direct physical motions that risk collisions or hardware damage.

Rhetorical Question: *Would you prefer discovering your code misreads sensor data when the robot is safely on a test bench, or during a live demo with obstacles?*

9.2.2 Unit Tests

1. **Definition:** Tests that **target small pieces** of code (functions, classes) in isolation.

2. **Goal:** Verify logic correctness without external dependencies (like hardware or complex frameworks).

3. **Tools:**

   - o **Python:** pytest, unittest modules.

- **C++**: gtest (Google Test).

4. **Examples**:

   - Checking a function that calculates wheel speeds from a linear.x, angular.z command.

   - Verifying a math library used for sensor filtering.

9.2.3 Integration Tests

1. **Definition**: Tests that **combine** multiple software components to ensure they work together.

2. **Goal**: Confirm nodes can communicate via ROS2 topics/services the way you expect.

3. **Examples**:

   - A test that launches a publisher node and a subscriber node to confirm messages reach the right topics.

   - Checking if your navigation stack can read a map and produce valid velocity commands.

Analogy: Integration tests are like verifying an entire band can play a song together, whereas unit tests check each musician can play their instrument in isolation.

9.2.4 Simulation Tests

1. **Definition**: Tests run in a **simulated environment** (Gazebo, Ignition, or custom simulators), allowing you

to see how your entire robot system behaves without physical hardware.

2. **Goal**: Evaluate higher-level behaviors (like navigation around obstacles) or multi-robot interactions in a reproducible, risk-free environment.

3. **ROS2**: You can automate simulation tests via launch files that spin up your simulation world, spawn the robot, run your nodes, and track outcomes (like whether the robot successfully reached a goal location).

9.2.5 Combining All Three

A robust testing strategy typically merges:

1. **Unit Tests** for code correctness.

2. **Integration Tests** for verifying node interactions.

3. **Simulation Tests** for system-level validation.

Continuous Integration (CI) pipelines can run these tests automatically whenever you push new code, ensuring no regression sneaks in.

9.2.6 Diagram 1: The Testing Pyramid for Robotics

```
+---------------------------------+
|   Simulation/System Tests |
| (Fewest, High Complexity,  |
|         Slower)            |
+---------------^-------------+
                |
+-----------------------------+
|     Integration Tests      |
| (Fewer, Moderate Complexity,|
|        Moderate Speed)     |
+---------------^-------------+
                |
+-----------------------------+
|        Unit Tests          |
| (Most Numerous, Low Complexity,|
|          Fast)             |
+-----------------------------+
```

9.3 Performance Optimization for Real-Time Systems

9.3.1 The Importance of Speed and Timing

A robot controlling motors or responding to sensor data may need to **process** that data in near real-time. High-latency or missed deadlines can cause the robot to overshoot, stutter, or fail to detect obstacles in time. **Performance** optimization is about ensuring code runs **fast** enough to meet these demands and remains stable under load.

Rhetorical Question: Would you trust a self-driving car that takes an extra second to recognize a pedestrian crossing?

9.3.2 Profiling and Bottleneck Identification

1. **Profilers**: Tools like Linux's perf, Visual Studio's profiler, or Python's cProfile identify where CPU cycles go.

2. **ROS2**: Additional overhead may come from message serialization/deserialization or large data streams. Use ros2 topic hz /topic to see if your node can publish/subscribe at the desired rate.

9.3.3 Real-Time Operating Systems (RTOS) and Scheduling

1. **RT-PREEMPT** Patches: Some robotics systems run on a real-time patched Linux kernel to guarantee scheduling latencies.

2. **DDS Tweaks**: Adjust QoS to reduce latency (avoid heavy reliability for high-speed sensor data if best-effort is acceptable).

3. **Thread Priorities**: Nodes controlling motors might get higher priority threads to ensure minimal jitter in control loops.

9.3.4 Memory and Network Considerations

1. **Buffer Sizes**: Large message queues can lead to delayed processing. Keep them sized properly to avoid message buildup.

2. **Zero-Copy**: Some ROS2 frameworks (like CycloneDDS) can do zero-copy data sharing under certain conditions, saving CPU time on big messages.

3. **Memory Leaks**: Unreleased resources degrade performance over time. Tools like valgrind in C++ or Python memory profilers help catch leaks.

9.3.5 System Architecture Optimization

- **Separate** heavy computations (e.g., vision inference) onto dedicated hardware or nodes.

- **Distribute** tasks across multiple machines if your robot's CPU or GPU is overloaded.

- **Caching** repeated calculations (like transformations or repeated math ops).

Analogy: Think of your robot's CPU as a traffic cop. If too many tasks converge at once, traffic jams occur, causing missed deadlines.

9.4 Documenting and Sharing Your Projects

9.4.1 Why Documentation Is Essential

Robotics involves **complex** hardware and software interactions. Without good documentation, the next person (or future you) working on the project might spend hours deciphering how code and wires connect.

Rhetorical Question: Ever found an old project folder with no README or clear instructions, leaving you guessing how it was set up?

9.4.2 Documentation Best Practices

1. **README** Files

   o Summarize the project's purpose, dependencies, build instructions, usage examples.

- o Keep it short, link to more detailed docs if needed.

2. **Code Comments**

- o Explain tricky logic or coordinate transformations.

- o Do not restate obvious lines (like "increment i"), but clarify "why" a line is crucial.

3. **Architecture Diagrams**

- o Show node communication, data flow, or hardware block diagrams.

- o **Diagram** can highlight how sensors feed into algorithms, culminating in motor commands.

4. **Auto-Generated Docs**

- o Tools like **Doxygen** (C++) or **Sphinx** (Python) can parse docstrings and produce HTML or PDF references.

- o Keep function/method docs concise but thorough.

9.4.3 Sharing and Collaboration

1. **Version Control**: Platforms like **GitHub** or **GitLab**.

2. **Issues and Pull Requests**: Track bugs, feature requests, and code reviews.

3. **Wiki/Project Pages:** Central place for user guides, advanced tutorials, and known issues.

4. **Community Involvement:** If open source, encourage others to fork, test, and contribute. If proprietary, maintain internal wikis or knowledge bases.

9.4.4 Ensuring Longevity

Projects that last beyond their creators' involvement typically have:

- **Clear Build Scripts** (like colcon build instructions).

- **Continuous Integration** that ensures building from scratch on a fresh environment.

- **Compatibility Docs** specifying ROS2 versions, OS versions, or hardware platforms tested.

9.5 Hands-On: Creating a Robust Testing Pipeline with ROS2 Tools

Now, let's tie everything together with a **hands-on** approach that sets up a **testing pipeline** for a sample ROS2 project. This pipeline will include **unit tests**, **integration tests**, and a **simulation test** to demonstrate how each layer can confirm your system's correctness and performance.

9.5.1 Project Overview

We'll assume a **simple mobile robot** project with two nodes:

1. **Motor Controller Node**: Subscribes to /cmd_vel for velocity commands and publishes /odom for wheel odometry.

2. **Obstacle Detection Node**: Subscribes to a mock LIDAR topic /scan and publishes a boolean /obstacle_detected.

We'll create:

- **Unit Tests**: For the math in each node (like converting velocity commands to wheel speeds).

- **Integration Tests**: Launch both nodes, verifying that a published /cmd_vel triggers correct /odom output.

- **Simulation Test**: In a minimal Gazebo environment, we confirm the robot can avoid a simple obstacle. We'll automate this with a single command (or CI pipeline) to run all tests.

9.5.2 Step 1: Setting Up the Package and Source Code

Assuming a ROS2 workspace ~/ros2_ws/src/, create a package:

```lua
ros2 pkg create --build-type ament_python mobile_robot_test
```

Inside mobile_robot_test/mobile_robot_test/, place:

1. **motor_controller.py**: A simplified node with logic for velocity->wheel speed.

2. **obstacle_detector.py**: Logic to read /scan and publish /obstacle_detected.

3. **init.py**: Makes the folder a Python module.

9.5.3 Step 2: Writing Unit Tests

Create test_motor_math.py:

python

```python
import unittest
from mobile_robot_test.motor_controller import
compute_wheel_speeds

class TestMotorMath(unittest.TestCase):
    def test_zero_velocity(self):
        left_speed, right_speed =
compute_wheel_speeds(0.0, 0.0)
        self.assertEqual(left_speed, 0.0)
        self.assertEqual(right_speed, 0.0)

    def test_forward_motion(self):
        left_speed, right_speed =
compute_wheel_speeds(1.0, 0.0)
        self.assertAlmostEqual(left_speed, 1.0,
places=2)
```

```
        self.assertAlmostEqual(right_speed, 1.0,
places=2)


if __name__ == '__main__':
    unittest.main()
```

1. **Compute Wheel Speeds** is a hypothetical function in motor_controller.py that returns (left_speed, right_speed).

2. This test verifies corner cases like zero velocity and straightforward forward motion.

9.5.4 Step 3: Writing Integration Tests with ROS2 Launch

Create test_integration_launch.py:

```python
import os
import pytest
import rclpy
from rclpy.node import Node
from std_msgs.msg import Float32
from geometry_msgs.msg import Twist
from launch import LaunchDescription
from launch_ros.actions import Node as LaunchNode
from launch_testing.actions import ReadyToTest


@pytest.mark.rostest
```

```python
def generate_test_description():
    motor_node = LaunchNode(
        package='mobile_robot_test',
        executable='motor_controller',
        name='motor_controller'
    )

    return LaunchDescription([
        motor_node,
        ReadyToTest()
    ])


@pytest.mark.rostest
class TestIntegration(Node):
    @classmethod
    def setUpClass(cls):
        rclpy.init()
        cls.node =
rclpy.create_node('test_integration_node')

    @classmethod
    def tearDownClass(cls):
        cls.node.destroy_node()
        rclpy.shutdown()

    def test_velocity_to_odom(self):
        # Publish a Twist and listen for Odom or
a speed topic
```

```
# ...
pass
```

1. **launch_testing** approach: We declare a launch file in code that starts the motor_controller node.

2. **test_velocity_to_odom**: We'd publish a /cmd_vel message and check if we get a corresponding /odom within a time limit.

Pro Tip: *The full code for integration tests can get more elaborate, but this snippet illustrates the pattern of launching nodes and verifying results.*

9.5.5 Step 4: Simulation Test in Gazebo

1. **Create** a minimal .world file with a box obstacle.

2. **Spawn** your robot and obstacle in a launch script:

```python
python


# test_sim.launch.py
from launch import LaunchDescription
from launch.actions import
IncludeLaunchDescription
from launch.launch_description_sources import
PythonLaunchDescriptionSource
import os

def generate_launch_description():
    # Path to the minimal world, containing a box
obstacle
```

```
    world_path = os.path.join(

get_package_share_directory('mobile_robot_test'),
        'worlds',
        'small_obstacle.world'
    )


    gazebo = IncludeLaunchDescription(
        PythonLaunchDescriptionSource(

[os.path.join(get_package_share_directory('gazebo
_ros'), 'launch', 'gazebo.launch.py')]
        ),
        launch_arguments={'world':
world_path}.items()
    )


    # Launch the robot's node(s)
    # ...
    return LaunchDescription([
        gazebo,
        # Node to spawn the robot,
        # Node for obstacle detector,
        # Possibly a test node that sets a goal,
    ])
```

2. **Automate** a test scenario: For instance, the test node publishes a goal velocity. If your obstacle detector sees

the box within X distance, it commands a stop. The test passes if the robot doesn't collide in simulation.

9.5.6 Step 5: One Command to Run All Tests

Write a test_all.sh script or add to setup.py:

bash

```
#!/bin/bash

colcon test --packages-select mobile_robot_test
colcon test-result --verbose
```

This ensures:

1. **Unit Tests** (like test_motor_math.py) run quickly in isolation.

2. **Integration Tests** with launch_testing run after.

3. **(Optional)** Simulation test if you include pytest or launch_testing scripts that start Gazebo.

CI Integration: On GitHub or GitLab, you can define a pipeline so that every commit triggers colcon build, then colcon test. No new code merges if tests fail.

9.5.7 Observing Results and Improving

- **Failing Tests:** If the unit test for wheel speed fails, you know your math changed or you introduced a bug.

- **Integration Test:** If it fails, your nodes aren't interacting properly—maybe a topic mismatch or logic error in the motor controller.

- **Simulation:** If the rover hits the box, your obstacle avoidance logic is lacking. Fix it, rerun. This feedback loop fosters **continuous improvement.**

Chapter Summary

This **Troubleshooting, Testing, and Continuous Improvement** chapter underscores the cyclical nature of robotics development: you **build,** you **test,** you **debug,** you **improve,** and the process repeats. Key takeaways:

1. **Common ROS2 Issues and Debugging**

   o Typos in topic names, mismatched message types, QoS incompatibilities, or domain ID misconfigurations frequently crop up.

   o Tools like ros2 topic, rqt_graph, RViz, logging, and methodical isolation can quickly pinpoint the culprit.

2. **Testing Methodologies**

   o **Unit Tests** ensure core functions do what they should in isolation.

   o **Integration Tests** confirm multiple nodes talk properly, with correct data flows.

- o **Simulation Tests** replicate real-world scenarios in a controlled environment, verifying system-level behavior.

3. **Performance Optimization**

- o Real-time constraints demand fast data handling, minimal latencies, and possibly real-time OS or scheduling.

- o Profilers identify bottlenecks. Careful QoS choices, memory management, and distributing workloads can resolve them.

4. **Documenting and Sharing**

- o Proper documentation (READMEs, diagrams, code comments) saves time and fosters collaboration.

- o Version control plus continuous integration ensures a stable, constantly improving codebase.

5. **Hands-On Testing Pipeline**

- o We walked through a **step-by-step** creation of unit tests, integration tests, and simulation tests for a minimal mobile robot project.

- o Combining them in a single colcon test or CI pipeline ensures comprehensive coverage and immediate feedback on code changes.

No Repetition: *While earlier chapters discussed various robotics fundamentals, here we zoomed in on **systematic***

debugging and *testing* *strategies—introducing new details on logging, QoS pitfalls, and the testing pyramid specifically for ROS2.*

Where to Go from Here?

1. **Advanced Debugging**: Explore advanced tools like GDB, LLDB, or Visual Studio Code's integrated debugging for stepping through node code line by line.

2. **Continuous Deployment**: Beyond testing, consider auto-deploying to your robot or test benches once code passes CI, bridging the gap between coding and real-world application.

3. **Hardware-in-the-Loop (HIL)**: For safety-critical robots, run tests that combine partial real hardware (motors, sensors) with simulated aspects, bridging the best of both testing worlds.

4. **Regression and Stress Testing**: Set up tests that run for hours or days, verifying stability under constant sensor streams or repeated tasks.

5. **Benchmarks**: Create performance benchmarks that measure CPU usage or response time under different loads, ensuring you meet real-time constraints.

Remember: an iterative approach to improvement means you never truly "finish" a robotics project—rather, you keep refining, optimizing, and testing, forging a path toward more

robust, efficient, and **satisfying** robot behaviors. Embrace the cycle of continuous improvement—your robot's reliability and your own engineering skills will thrive as a result.

Chapter 10: Case Studies and Practical Applications

So far in this book, we've seen how **ROS2** (Robot Operating System 2) lays the groundwork for modular, scalable, and robust robotics applications. But how does all this translate into actual **real-world** impact? In this chapter, we'll explore **case studies** that highlight the versatility and power of ROS2 across different industries and use cases. Whether it's assisting patients in a hospital, boosting factory throughput, optimizing warehouses, or tackling emerging domains like agriculture, ROS2 provides a unifying framework for managing sensors, controlling motion, and coordinating multiple robots.

We'll conclude with a **hands-on** mini case study in which you'll see how to recreate a simple **Warehouse AGV** scenario in simulation—reinforcing the chapter's central message: **ROS2** can transform almost any environment that benefits from automated, intelligent solutions.

10.1 ROS2 in Healthcare: Assistive Robots

10.1.1 Why Healthcare Needs Robotics

Healthcare is multifaceted—ranging from busy hospital wards to home-based patient care. Robotics can alleviate mundane tasks, reduce caregiver workload, and enhance patient safety. As medical facilities face staff shortages or increased patient demands, assistive robots help:

1. **Deliver medicines** or supplies,

2. **Guide patients** to different departments,

3. **Monitor vitals** in telemedicine contexts,

4. **Assist in patient transfer** or mobility.

Rhetorical Question: Have you ever watched nurses or aides ferry supplies across sprawling hospital floors? Doesn't it make sense for a robot to handle these repetitive tasks, freeing humans for patient-centered care?

10.1.2 Example: ROS2-Driven Hospital Delivery Robot

Case Study: A mid-sized hospital deployed a **ROS2-based** autonomous mobile robot (AMR) to shuttle medical equipment between surgical theaters and storage rooms. Here's how it works:

1. **SLAM and Map:** Technicians walked the robot around corridors during off-peak hours, enabling it to build a 2D map with LIDAR.

2. **Navigation Stack:** Once the map was set, the **ROS2 navigation stack** (nav2) handled path planning.

3. **Task Scheduling:** Nurses or staff used a tablet UI, specifying pickup points and destinations.

4. **Elevator Integration:** The robot used a **ROS2 service** that pings the building's "smart elevator" system, ensuring the door opens at the correct floor.

Impact:

- The hospital reported a **25% reduction** in staff time spent on retrieving supplies.

- Fewer disruptions in patient-care tasks.

- The robot also provided real-time location data to the central system, aiding hospital logistics.

10.1.3 Key ROS2 Features for Healthcare

1. **Security and HIPAA Compliance:** Sensitive patient data might traverse a robot's sensors or servers. ROS2's DDS can incorporate encryption and authentication, ensuring minimal risk of data leaks.

2. **Reliable QoS:** Frequent Wi-Fi disruptions in large buildings demand robust communication. A "reliable"

Quality of Service ensures messages persist until successfully received.

3. **Integration with IoT Devices:** The robot can subscribe to hospital "smart building" systems or RFID trackers for advanced logistics.

Diagram 1: Hospital Delivery Robot Workflow

```
+------------------------------------------------------------------+
|                       Hospital Floor Plan                        |
+------------------------------------------------------------------+
                                                                  |
  +--------------+       +--------------------+      +----------------+ /
  | Pharmacy     |       | Operating Theatre|      | Supply Room    |  |
  | (Room 101)   |       |   (Room 202)     |      |  (Room 303)    |  |
  +-------+------+       +--------------------+      +----------------+ /
         |                        |                        |
         |                        |                        |
         |                        |                        |
         |                        |                        |
         |                        |                        |
         |                        |                        |
  +------+------+       +---------v--------+      +---------v--------+ /
  | Staff Tablet | <------ | ROS2 Service  | -------> | Elevator       | /
  | (Issuing    |        | (Task Requests)  |      | Integration Node| |
  | Tasks)      |        +------------------+      +--------+--------+ /
  +-------------+                                          /         /
                                                          |         |
                                                          |         |
                                          +---------------v---------+ /
                                          |     Building Controls   | |
                                          | (Elevator Controls, Lighting,  | |
                                          |      HVAC, etc.)        | |
                                          +-------------------------+ /
                                                                    |
```

```
+------------------------------------------------+      /
|                                                |      |
|   Mobile Delivery Robot (R1)                   |      |
|   +--------------------------------+           |      /
|   |          [ R1 ]                |           |      /
|   +----------------+---------------+           |      /
|                    |                           |      |
|                    |                           |      |
|   +----------------v-----------+               |      |
|   |     ROS2 Navigation        |               |      |
|   |        Node                |               |      |
|   +----------------------------+               |      /
|                    |                           |      |
|                    |                           |      |
|   +----------------v-----------+               |      /
|   |     Sensor Inputs          |               |      |
|   |  (LIDAR, Camera, etc.)     |               |      |
|   +----------------------------+               |      |
+------------------------------------------------+      /
|                                                       |
|                                                       |
|                                                       |
+-------------------------------------------------------+
|                      Legend                           |
|  [ R1 ]        : Mobile Delivery Robot                |
|  Arrows        : Data Flow / Task Assignments         |
|  Boxes         : Key Components and Nodes             |
|  Icons         : Devices (Robots, Tablets)            |
+-------------------------------------------------------+
```

10.2 ROS2 in Manufacturing: Automation and Production Lines

10.2.1 Evolution of Automation

Modern factories go well beyond conveyor belts and static robotic arms. Flexibility is key—production lines might shift from one product to another daily, or multiple lines might converge to assemble complex items. **ROS2** adds a new dimension:

1. **Modular Machines**: Each robotic arm or mobile platform runs its own ROS2 node, easily reconfigurable or replaceable.

2. **Cross-Vendor Interoperability**: Factories often house equipment from different manufacturers. ROS2's open source nature fosters cross-device communication.

10.2.2 Case Study: Robot Arm Assembly Line with Real-Time Control

Company X implemented a **ROS2-based** solution for an **assembly line** manufacturing consumer electronics. Key steps:

1. **Camera Node**: A vision system above the conveyor detects part orientation, publishing part location on /part_pose.

2. **Robotic Arm Node:** Subscribes to /part_pose, uses an **inverse kinematics** service to compute safe pick-up angles, then picks and places the part on a fixture.

3. **Mobile Robot Node:** Delivers finished sub-assemblies to the next station using nav2.

Real-Time Challenges:

- High throughput demands sub-second detection-to-action cycles.

- **QoS** settings (best-effort vs. reliable) must be carefully chosen for each sensor or control stream.

- A **hardware-accelerated** edge device (NVIDIA Jetson or Intel Movidius) assists with real-time image processing.

Results:

- **50% faster** part throughput, **reduced error rates** from misalignment.

- The management praised the system's flexibility—new product lines only require slight retuning of the vision node or the pick-and-place pipeline.

10.2.3 Common Patterns in Manufacturing with ROS2

- **Synchronization:** Multiple robots or stages rely on messages like "Station 1 done, Station 2 start."

- **Safety Fences**: A ROS2 "safety node" monitors intrusion sensors or E-stop signals, instantly halting operations if a human crosses into the danger zone.

- **Fleet of Mobile Robots**: Instead of fixed conveyors, some factories deploy small "cart-like" AGVs using ROS2 to ferry materials.

Diagram 2: Production Line with ROS2 Nodes

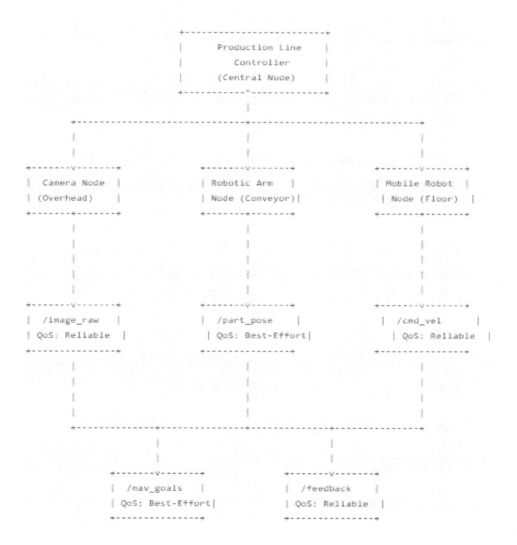

10.3 ROS2 in Logistics: Warehouse AGVs (Automated Guided Vehicles)

10.3.1 The Rise of AGVs and AMRs

The logistics sector—warehouse operations, distribution centers, e-commerce fulfillment—relies heavily on **autonomous vehicles** to reduce manual labor and speed up deliveries. Two broad categories:

1. **AGVs (Automated Guided Vehicles)**: Typically follow fixed paths (wires or magnetic strips).

2. **AMRs (Autonomous Mobile Robots)**: Rely on onboard sensors and dynamic navigation to roam freely.

ROS2 helps unify the software stacks for both, letting developers reuse navigation, mapping, and fleet management components across platforms.

Rhetorical Question: Have you ever wondered how an online retailer can ship items so rapidly? Automated picking and AGVs are a massive part of the secret.

10.3.2 Case Study: Large E-Commerce Warehouse

A major e-commerce retailer integrated **ROS2** into their second-generation warehouse robots:

1. **Fleet Manager Node:** Assigns tasks to each robot (like retrieving order #123 from aisle B4).

2. **Per-Robot Node:** Each AMR uses a LIDAR or depth camera to avoid collisions and localize on a 2D map.

3. **Cloud Monitoring:** Periodically, the robot uploads logs and sensor snapshots for big data analysis (fault detection, route optimization).

Key Results:

- **75% reduction** in human walking time, enabling human pickers to remain in a centralized picking station while robots bring items.

- Improved **safety:** Fewer forklift-human collisions, as the robots automatically yield or reroute.

- Real-time changes: If the warehouse layout changes (temporary shelves or new racks), the system updates global and local maps accordingly.

10.3.3 ROS2 Advantages in Logistics

- **Nav2:** The ROS2 navigation stack is well-suited for dynamic obstacle avoidance, ephemeral structures, and route replanning.

- **Distributed Architecture:** Each robot can run its own node set, but the central server can track and coordinate the entire fleet.

- **Scalability**: Additional robots can be introduced with minimal reconfiguration, discovering relevant topics or services automatically.

10.3.4 Integration with WMS (Warehouse Management Systems)

Often, these robots must interface with:

- **ERP** (Enterprise Resource Planning) or **WMS** software.

- Through a **ROS2 service** or custom adapter, real-time data about inventory levels or picking schedules flows to the robots, guiding them to specific bin locations.

10.4 Emerging Use Cases (Agriculture, Search-and-Rescue, and More)

10.4.1 Agriculture

1. **Crop Monitoring**: Small rovers or drones traverse fields, collecting plant health data (e.g., NDVI indices) or detecting weeds.

2. **Precision Spraying**: Robots identify weeds vs. crops, applying pesticides only where needed.

3. **Harvesting**: Robotic arms carefully pick fruits or vegetables without damaging them, guided by vision nodes in ROS2.

Real-World Example: In orchard management, a **ROS2-based** orchard rover maps orchard rows, measuring fruit ripeness with near-infrared sensors. The system's distributed architecture allows plugging in additional sensors or robots for large-scale orchard coverage.

10.4.2 Search-and-Rescue

1. **Disaster Zones**: A track-based robot or drone uses a LIDAR + camera setup for mapping rubble.

2. **Autonomous Exploration**: A node that detects open pathways vs. blocked zones and autonomously ventures deeper, searching for survivors.

3. **Multi-Robot Collaboration**: Swarms of small ground robots or UAVs share partial maps, collectively building situational awareness for rescue teams.

ROS2 Value: Tools like multi-map merging or distributed SLAM let robots quickly piece together unknown terrains. The robust communication system can function in partially connected networks (some robots might temporarily lose contact but resync upon rejoining the network).

10.4.3 Other Emerging Applications

- **Entertainment**: Theme parks or interactive shows use ROS2 for choreographing large numbers of mobile platforms or animatronics.

- **Hospitality:** Hotel delivery bots or greeter robots that rely on local vision plus cloud-based AI, integrated with a ROS2 backbone.

- **Construction:** Wheeled or legged robots scanning worksites for progress monitoring or performing 3D printing of structures onsite.

Rhetorical Question: If you can coordinate dozens of AGVs in a warehouse, why not do the same for a construction site, orchard, or an entire campus?

Matrix Overview

Industry	Navigation (nav2)	Perception (OpenCV, Sensor Fusion)	Multi-Robot Coordination (Fleet Manager Nodes)	Cloud Integration / Data Analytics
Agriculture	✓	✓	✓	✓
Search & Rescue (S&R)	✓	✓	✓	✓
Entertainment	✓	✓	✓	✓
Construction	✓	✓	✓	✓
Manufacturing	✓	✓	✓	✓
Healthcare	✓	✓	✓	✓
Logistics & Warehousing	✓	✓	✓	✓

10.5 Hands-On: Recreating a Mini Case Study for a Warehouse AGV

As a **hands-on** exercise, let's simulate a **basic warehouse AGV** scenario in ROS2, offering a small-scale demonstration of how logistics robots handle tasks like path following, obstacle avoidance, and "pickup-delivery" cycles.

10.5.1 Project Overview

1. **Objective**: Create a minimal "warehouse" simulation in **Gazebo** (or Ignition). Place a small mobile robot (AGV) that can deliver items from a "loading station" to a "drop-off station."

2. **ROS2**: We'll rely on **nav2** for path planning and obstacle avoidance, and a simplified "task manager" node for instructions.

3. **Focus**: Emphasizing the main concepts: mapping, route planning, and an example of "pickup" and "drop-off" logic.

10.5.2 Step 1: Setting Up the Simulated Warehouse

1. **Install** the relevant Gazebo or Ignition packages for your ROS2 distribution.

2. **Create** a .world file that includes:

- A rectangular space simulating a small warehouse floor.

- A few static boxes or shelves as obstacles.

- A "loading station" (Station A) and a "drop-off station" (Station B).

3. **Optional:** A custom texture or environment that mimics a warehouse floor.

Example (conceptual snippet in SDF or URDF):

```xml
<model name="Shelf1">
  <!-- position, collision elements, etc. -->
</model>
<model name="Shelf2">
  <!-- second shelf -->
</model>
<model name="FloorMarkings">
  <!-- lines or markings on the floor for
aesthetics -->
</model>
```

Tip: The simpler your environment, the easier debugging. You can add complexity (more shelves, dynamic obstacles) later.

10.5.3 Step 2: Configuring Your AGV

We'll assume:

- **Differential Drive** or Ackermann steering.

- A **LIDAR** sensor for obstacle detection.

- **Odometry** from wheel encoders.

- A URDF file describing geometry, mass, sensor plugins, etc.

Launch File snippet (conceptual):

```python
from launch import LaunchDescription
from launch.actions import
IncludeLaunchDescription
from launch.launch_description_sources import
PythonLaunchDescriptionSource
import os

def generate_launch_description():
    # Path to the warehouse world
    warehouse_world = os.path.join(

get_package_share_directory('mini_agv_sim'),
        'worlds',
        'warehouse.world'
    )
```

```
# Launch Gazebo
gazebo = IncludeLaunchDescription(
    PythonLaunchDescriptionSource([

os.path.join(get_package_share_directory('gazebo_
ros'), 'launch', 'gazebo.launch.py')
    ]),
    launch_arguments={'world':
warehouse_world}.items()
)


# Spawn the AGV
# ...
return LaunchDescription([
    gazebo,
    # spawn code, nav2, etc.
])
```

10.5.4 Step 3: Setting Up nav2 (Navigation Stack)

1. **Map:** If your warehouse is static, you can manually create a 2D occupancy grid using a local SLAM approach or by exporting from a known layout.

2. **nav2** Configuration**: A YAML file controlling costmap parameters, inflation radius, sensor topics, etc.

3. **Launch nav2**: Typically includes map_server, planner_server, controller_server, and bt_navigator.

Example: my_nav2_params.yaml might define:

```yaml
amcl:
  ros__parameters:
    max_particles: 500
    laser_scan_topic: /scan

controller_server:
  ros__parameters:
    min_vel_x: 0.0
    max_vel_x: 0.5
    # ...
```

10.5.5 Step 4: Task Manager Node

We want a simple "pickup and deliver" cycle:

1. The node listens on /task_cmd.

2. If it receives "pickup," it sets a **navigation goal** to Station A. Once the AGV arrives, it simulates loading items (maybe a short delay).

3. Next, it sets a goal to Station B. Once the robot arrives, it simulates unloading.

4. The cycle repeats or ends.

Pseudo-Code:

```python
python


class WarehouseTaskManager(Node):
    def __init__(self):


super().__init__('warehouse_task_manager')
        self.nav_client = ActionClient(self,
NavigateToPose, 'navigate_to_pose')
        self.subscription =
self.create_subscription(String, '/task_cmd',
self.task_callback, 10)


    def task_callback(self, msg):
        if msg.data == "pickup":
            # navigate to station A
            # wait for feedback
            # simulate load
            # navigate to station B
            # simulate unload
```

10.5.6 Step 5: Running the Scenario

1. **Terminal A:**

```
ros2 launch mini_agv_sim warehouse_sim.launch.py
```
   o Loads Gazebo, spawns the AGV, starts nav2.

2. **Terminal B:**

```arduino

ros2 run mini_agv_sim warehouse_task_manager
Terminal C:
rust


ros2 topic pub /task_cmd std_msgs/String "data:
'pickup'"
```

- o The AGV should move to Station A, wait, then go to Station B.

Observations:

- If the AGV senses shelves or boxes in its path, it reroutes.

- You can place extra obstacles or dynamically move them to test local planner adaptability.

***Rhetorical Question**: Doesn't this small simulation echo the same principles used by giant e-commerce warehouses?*

10.5.7 Possible Enhancements

- **Integrate** a camera for barcodes or fiducial markers.

- **Use** a multi-robot scenario (two AGVs) with a shared "task allocation" system.

- **Add** "charging stations" where the robot docks when low on battery, bridging power management.

Chapter Summary

This **Case Studies and Practical Applications** chapter showcases how **ROS2** powers real-world robotics across various fields, from assisting hospital staff to orchestrating entire fleets of warehouse AGVs. We've seen how **modular architecture** and **standardized messaging** enable:

1. **Healthcare**: Autonomous delivery robots, telepresence bots, or patient-assistive devices.

2. **Manufacturing**: Real-time pick-and-place arms, flexible production lines, and integrated AGVs for shop-floor logistics.

3. **Logistics**: Large e-commerce facilities with fleets of AMRs, all coordinated under a ROS2-based central server.

4. **Emerging Domains**: Agriculture (crop monitoring, precision spraying), search-and-rescue (collaborative mapping in disaster zones), and beyond.

5. **Hands-On Mini AGV**: A demonstration of building a small "warehouse" scenario in simulation, from creating a 2D map to controlling an autonomous routine that picks up and drops off items.

*No Repetition: Instead of rehashing earlier chapters' fundamentals, we focused here on **practical, domain-specific** details and how organizations adopt ROS2 to solve real-life challenges.*

Where to Go from Here?

1. **Deep Dives**: If you're particularly interested in healthcare or industrial automation, follow relevant research or standardization efforts (e.g., ISO standards for medical devices).

2. **Advanced Fleet Management**: Explore scheduling algorithms, conflict resolution, or cloud-based multi-factory coordination.

3. **Scaling**: Move from single robots to entire **multi-robot** fleets, using advanced **ROS2** discovery configurations or bridging multiple networks.

4. **Integration with AI**: Incorporate advanced object detection or reinforcement learning for tasks like dynamic picking, fruit harvesting, or search-and-rescue in cluttered environments.

5. **Commercial Platforms**: Investigate specialized hardware that supports ROS2 out-of-the-box (like certain mobile bases or robotic arms), accelerating deployment.

In short, ROS2's success across so many domains underscores a simple truth: a **flexible** and **reliable** robotic framework can adapt to almost any setting, whether you're delivering bandages in a hospital corridor or sorting packages in a thousand-square-foot warehouse. By harnessing the case study insights and hands-on experience

from this chapter, you can bring your own robotics visions—
no matter how large or small—closer to reality.

Chapter 11: Looking Ahead — Robotics Trends and Ongoing Innovation

Robotics is a field in perpetual motion, blending **software, hardware, and intelligence** in ways that continually redefine what's possible. Where we once imagined robots only in sci-fi, we now see them **driving** cars, **delivering** goods, **assisting** in surgeries, and **traversing** the surfaces of other planets. As we arrive at the closing chapter of this book, it's time to lift our gaze from present-day projects to the **innovations and trends** set to shape the next era of robotics.

In this chapter, we'll explore:

1. **The Future of ROS2**: Ongoing development of the ecosystem, community support, and version roadmaps.

2. **Artificial Intelligence and Robotics**: How next-generation autonomy, powered by AI, is transforming robotic capabilities.

3. **Ethical and Societal Considerations**: Balancing innovation with responsibility in a world where robots increasingly intersect with daily life.

4. **Final Thoughts and Further Resources**: Offering concluding perspectives and pointers for continued learning.

5. **Hands-On: Setting Up Your Personal Robotics Roadmap**: A practical exercise to help you chart a course forward, whether you're a hobbyist, student, or professional.

11.1 The Future of ROS2: Ecosystem Growth and Support

11.1.1 Ongoing Development: A Vibrant Community

ROS2 has traveled a swift trajectory. Originally an evolution of the classic ROS1, it introduced **reliability, security, and flexibility** features designed for industrial and real-time scenarios. Today, the ROS2 ecosystem is more than just a software framework:

- **Global Community**: Thousands of developers, researchers, and companies contribute code, report issues, and create tutorials.

- **Regular Distributions**: Names like Foxy, Galactic, Humble, Iron—each with new features and extended support lifecycles.

- **Cross-Platform Maturity**: From Ubuntu Linux to Windows and macOS, plus microcontroller-focused subsets (Micro-ROS), each iteration brings improved stability and performance.

Rhetorical Question: Ever wonder how so many disparate robots—drones, arms, rovers—run the "same" system? The secret lies in ROS2's open, modular architecture and the unstoppable momentum of its open-source community.

11.1.2 New Frontiers: WebAssembly, Micro-ROS, and More

1. **WebAssembly Integration**: Some developers are exploring ways to run parts of ROS2 in a **web browser** or on resource-limited devices, letting you manage robotic data in real time via web-based dashboards.

2. **Micro-ROS**: Tailored for embedded hardware with minimal resources (like microcontrollers). This expansion means even the smallest sensors or actuators can speak the same language as large, computationally heavy robots.

3. **Security and Encryption**: Expect further improvements in **DDS** (Data Distribution Service) encryption, authentication, and secure real-time messaging, especially in mission-critical or medical robotics domains.

11.1.3 Growing Industry Adoption

ROS2 is now an **industry standard** in many sectors:

- **Automotive**: Self-driving or driver-assist platforms rely on ROS2 to integrate sensors, plan paths, and run advanced AI modules.

- **Aerospace**: Research labs use ROS2 for experimental drones, planetary rovers, or satellite-servicing robots.

- **Manufacturing**: A continuing shift from proprietary industrial protocols to open frameworks sees ROS2 bridging the gap among diverse machines.

11.2 Artificial Intelligence and Robotics: Next-Generation Autonomy

11.2.1 The AI-Robotics Convergence

Robots can't achieve **true autonomy** without sophisticated intelligence. Previously, developers wrote endless rules or heuristics for each task, but the era of **machine learning**—particularly deep learning and reinforcement learning—transformed robotics from "if-else" driven systems to ones that **learn** from data and adapt to unforeseen conditions.

*Analogy: Think of the shift like going from a carefully choreographed dance to **improvisational jazz**—the robot's* *"moves" become fluid, responding to dynamic changes in the environment.*

11.2.2 Machine Learning Methods Shaping Robotics

1. **Computer Vision**: Convolutional neural networks (CNNs) for object detection, SLAM enhancements, or scene understanding.

2. **Reinforcement Learning**: Agents learn by trial and error, receiving "rewards" for good actions—like stable walking for legged robots or optimized route selection.

3. **Natural Language Processing (NLP)**: As voice interfaces and textual instructions become more common, robots can parse and execute commands in everyday language.

4. **Federated Learning**: Multiple robots in different locations collectively train a shared model without centralized data (useful for privacy in healthcare or remote sites).

11.2.3 Pushing Boundaries: Human-Robot Collaboration

Next-gen AI fosters deeper collaboration between humans and robots:

- **Shared Autonomy:** A user teleoperates a robot at a high level, while the robot fills in details (like obstacle avoidance).

- **Intent Prediction:** AI might predict the user's intentions by analyzing gaze, gestures, or partial voice commands.

- **Adaptive Control:** A robot that automatically modifies its approach if it senses user discomfort or changing environment constraints.

11.3 Ethical and Societal Considerations in Robotics

11.3.1 The Dual-Edged Sword of Automation

As robots and AI become more pervasive, society faces complex questions:

1. **Job Displacement:** Automated systems can replace repetitive or hazardous jobs, but also create new roles (robot maintenance, data science). The transition can be disruptive if not carefully managed.

2. **Privacy:** Robots collecting video or sensor data in public or private spaces must address privacy regulations, especially in healthcare or home care scenarios.

3. **Bias in AI**: If a robot's vision or decision algorithm is trained on biased data, it may inadvertently treat certain individuals or scenarios differently, raising fairness concerns.

Rhetorical Question: If your home-care robot inadvertently uploads personal living habits to the cloud, who should control that data, and how can we ensure it stays secure?

11.3.2 Safety and Accountability

When robots cause harm—like an autonomous vehicle crash—who is responsible? Potential answers:

- **Manufacturer** (hardware design flaw),
- **Software Vendor** (algorithmic error),
- **Operator** (misuse or failing to maintain the system).

This leads to calls for clear **regulation, standards**, and **certifications** ensuring robots meet rigorous safety checks before deployment.

11.3.3 Human-Robot Interaction (HRI)

Designing ethical and socially accepted robots involves:

1. **Transparent Interactions**: Indicating intentions through LED signals, voice prompts, or body language (in the case of humanoids).

2. **Emotional Intelligence**: Some advanced robots in eldercare or therapy contexts can sense emotional

cues—like frustration or sadness—and respond helpfully.

3. **Inclusion and Accessibility**: Robots must accommodate diverse human abilities, languages, and cultural contexts.

11.3.4 Fostering Responsible Innovation

Collaborative dialogues among government agencies, nonprofits, academia, and industry can produce frameworks that encourage innovation while respecting human rights. Real progress emerges when robotics companies adopt **Privacy-by-Design** and **Ethics-by-Design** principles, anticipating potential misuses or harms.

11.4 Final Thoughts and Further Resources

11.4.1 Conclusion: The Endless Frontier

Throughout this book, we've highlighted how **ROS2** empowers roboticists to build everything from simple mobile rovers to advanced multi-robot fleets. As **hardware** miniaturizes and **AI** advances, robotics becomes more **powerful, versatile,** and **ubiquitous**. While the journey is far from simple—there are real-world challenges in reliability, safety, and ethics—the potential is breathtaking.

Analogy: *Robotics is the next frontier of computing, akin to the personal computer revolution in the 1980s or the* *internet explosion of the 1990s. Each new milestone reveals fresh possibilities.*

11.4.2 Further Resources

- **ROS Discourse:** An official forum where developers and hobbyists share tips, solutions, and announcements.

- **ROS2 Documentation:** Official docs at docs.ros.org—regularly updated with new distributions, API references, and tutorials.

- **GitHub Repositories:** Thousands of open-source packages for specialized sensors, advanced algorithms, or entire robot solutions.

- **Conferences and Events: ROSCon, IROS, ICRA**—major gatherings to see the latest robotics research and network with experts.

11.4.3 Lifelong Learning

Robotics is a domain of perpetual growth. Keep:

1. **Experimenting:** Tinker with new sensors or AI algorithms.

2. **Contributing:** Publish your packages, bug fixes, or tutorials.

3. **Staying Curious:** Follow academic papers, video lectures, or industry news.

Tip: *Weekly or monthly scanning of new robotics GitHub projects can spark ideas for your own. Innovations often emerge from unexpected corners of the community.*

11.5 Hands-On: Setting Up Your Personal Robotics Roadmap

To wrap up, let's do a **step-by-step** exercise to design your **personal robotics roadmap**. This roadmap helps you identify your **goals**, needed **skills**, and **action plan**. Whether you're a newcomer or a seasoned engineer pivoting to advanced autonomy, a structured plan keeps you motivated and efficient.

11.5.1 Step 1: Identify Your Goals

Ask yourself:

1. **What intrigues you most about robotics?** (Examples: swarm systems, humanoid arms, agricultural drones, or social robots.)

2. **Do you prefer hardware building or software/AI?** (Or a balanced mix?)

3. **Short-Term vs. Long-Term:** Maybe short-term you want to master basic navigation, while long-term you aim to build a commercial product or pursue advanced research.

*Action: Draft a short paragraph describing your **robotics dream**—the reason you're drawn to the field.*

11.5.2 Step 2: Assess Current Skills

Be honest about your:

- **Programming proficiency** (Python, C++).

- **Math foundation** (linear algebra, geometry for kinematics).

- **Electronics/hardware** knowledge (wiring, sensors).

- **Domain knowledge** (e.g., if you want to do surgical robotics, do you understand the medical environment?).

Action: Create a 2-column table:

Skill Category	Current Level
Programming	Intermediate (Python, some C++)
Math & Kinematics	Basic
Electronics	Beginner
Domain Knowledge	...

This baseline helps focus your learning plan.

11.5.3 Step 3: Research and Resource Collection

For each skill gap:

1. **Find a course or tutorial**: For math, maybe an online course in linear algebra. For electronics, a beginner Arduino/embedded systems series.

2. **Pick relevant ROS2 tutorials**: If you plan to use advanced navigation, look for official nav2 or multi-robot tutorials.

3. **Bookmark** reference sites or GitHub repos that align with your goals.

Action: Consolidate these resources in a text document or mind map. Label them by priority (must-learn soon vs. optional/future).

11.5.4 Step 4: Create a Timeline

Set **realistic milestones**. For example:

1. **Month 1**: Complete a "Beginner's Python for Robotics" tutorial.

2. **Month 2**: Build a small differential-drive robot with a basic sensor, run a ROS2 nav tutorial.

3. **Month 3-4**: Explore an advanced topic (like AI-based object detection).

4. **Month 5+**: Start a "portfolio project" aligning with your dream application.

Tip: Keep intervals short enough to maintain motivation, but not so short that you become overwhelmed.

11.5.5 Step 5: Document Progress and Reflect

1. **Logbooks**: Maintain a notebook or digital journal with daily or weekly notes—what you accomplished, obstacles faced, solutions found.

2. **Demo Videos**: If comfortable, record short clips of your robot in action for personal reflection or public sharing.

3. **Adjust**: If a resource or approach isn't helpful, pivot. The roadmap is a living plan.

11.5.6 Step 6: Community and Mentors

Strong communities accelerate your learning:

- **Join** local robotics meetups or online groups.

- **Seek a mentor**—someone with experience in your target domain.

- **Offer help**: Answer forum questions, write how-to guides. Teaching others cements your own knowledge.

Chapter Summary

In this **forward-looking** chapter, we explored the **trajectory** of robotics and how **ROS2** continues to evolve, linking cutting-edge AI with secure, scalable systems. Key sections included:

1. **The Future of ROS2**:

   - Ongoing version releases, robust community support, and expansions like micro-ROS for embedded devices.

   - Industrial adoption leading to cross-vendor interoperability.

2. **Artificial Intelligence and Robotics**:

   - Next-generation autonomy driven by machine learning, reinforcement learning, and AI-based perception.

   - Blurring lines between teleoperation and full autonomy, with robots increasingly "learning" from data and environment feedback.

3. **Ethical and Societal Considerations**:

   - Balancing automation's benefits with concerns about privacy, job displacement, bias, and accountability.

   - Designing inclusive, safe, and transparent robot behaviors fosters trust and ensures responsible innovation.

4. **Final Thoughts and Further Resources:**

   o Encouragement to keep experimenting, contributing, and exploring advanced topics in ROS2.

   o Listing official documentation, community forums, and events as potential next steps.

5. **Hands-On: Setting Up Your Personal Robotics Roadmap:**

   o **Step-by-step** approach for self-assessment, goal setting, resource gathering, timeline creation, and continuous self-review.

   o Encouragement to engage with mentors, communities, and real-world projects for deeper learning.

*No Repetition: Rather than rehash prior content on ROS2 fundamentals, we specifically focused on **futuristic trends**— the forward momentum of robotics, deeper AI integrations, ethical dialogues, and personal growth strategies.*

A Final Word

Robotics stands at the intersection of **science, engineering, and imagination.** By embracing **continuous learning**, seeking out community collaboration, and never forgetting the human dimension—our dreams, our ethics, our needs—you can help shape the next wave of innovation. Whether you build small rovers in a home workshop or design industrial-scale solutions in a major corporation, **ROS2** is your ally and your gateway to boundless possibilities.

Stay curious, stay creative—and let your robotics journey continue!

Appendices

Table of Contents

1. **Appendix A**: Glossary of Robotics and ROS2 Terms

2. **Appendix B**: Additional Python Resources and Tutorials

3. **Appendix C**: Recommended Tools, Libraries, and Hardware Vendors

4. **Appendix D**: Troubleshooting Reference Cheat Sheets

Appendix A: Glossary of Robotics and ROS2 Terms

As you've worked through this book, you've encountered numerous **terms** related to **robotics**, **ROS2**, and **AI**. This appendix consolidates the most important definitions into a quick-reference **glossary**. Keep in mind that each term appears in **plain language**, ensuring immediate clarity without needing to re-read entire chapters.

A.1 Action

- **Definition**: In ROS2, an Action is a **long-running task** that provides **feedback** during execution and ends with a final **result**.

- **Example:** A robot arm picking a box might periodically report progress ("50% done," "70% done") and then signal a success or failure at the end.

A.2 Actuator

- **Definition:** A **component** (motor, servo) that **turns electrical signals** into **physical motion**.

- **Analogy:** Think of an actuator like your arm's muscles; signals from your nerves become actual limb movements.

A.3 Autonomy

- **Definition:** The robot's ability to **make decisions** and **execute tasks** with minimal or no human intervention.

- **Rhetorical Question:** Does complete autonomy mean zero oversight? Not necessarily—some tasks still rely on high-level human guidance.

A.4 Behavior Tree

- **Definition:** A **hierarchical structure** for controlling robot actions, particularly in navigation or complex tasks. Each node represents a decision, condition, or action.

- **Why It Matters:** Behavior trees allow simpler debugging and modular logic building compared to monolithic if-else blocks.

A.5 Costmap

- **Definition**: A **grid** or data structure in ROS2's Navigation Stack that represents how "costly" or risky it is for a robot to enter a particular cell, based on obstacles.

- **Visual Aid**: Often displayed in RViz as a color-coded map where red indicates high cost (walls, hazards).

A.6 DDS (Data Distribution Service)

- **Definition**: A **communication protocol** under ROS2's hood, handling discovery and data exchange among nodes.

- **Analogy**: DDS is like a flexible postal system ensuring each node can find the others and deliver messages reliably (or best-effort, if you prefer).

A.7 Differential Drive

- **Definition**: A drive system with **two separately powered wheels** on a single axis, often with a caster wheel in back or front.

- **Example**: Many entry-level mobile robots use this design, offering in-place turning.

A.8 Domain ID

- **Definition**: A numerical identifier that groups ROS2 nodes so they discover one another only within that domain.

- **Use:** In multi-robot labs, each robot might have a unique domain ID to avoid cross-talk.

A.9 Frame (tf2)

- **Definition:** A **coordinate system** attached to a robot part, sensor, or environment.

- **Example:** base_link (robot's main frame), camera_link (camera frame). tf2 transforms let you convert points between frames.

A.10 Holonomic Drive

- **Definition:** A drive system (often using omni or mecanum wheels) that can move in **any direction** without rotating first.

- **Analogy:** Like an office chair that can glide sideways, forward, backward, or rotate independently.

A.11 IMU (Inertial Measurement Unit)

- **Definition:** A sensor combining **accelerometers** and **gyroscopes** (and sometimes a magnetometer) to track orientation and acceleration.

- **Why It's Important:** Provides essential data for stable navigation, especially on uneven terrain.

A.12 Launch File

- **Definition:** A Python script or XML file that **starts** multiple ROS2 nodes (and configurations) at once.

- **Rhetorical Question**: Tired of opening multiple terminals for each node? A launch file is your best friend.

A.13 Navigation Stack (nav2)

- **Definition**: A collection of ROS2 packages providing **local and global path planning**, obstacle avoidance, and map handling.

- **Use**: Commonly used for autonomous mobile robots in indoor or structured environments.

A.14 Node

- **Definition**: A **process** in ROS2 that performs specific tasks, such as reading sensor data or controlling motors.

- **Core Idea**: Splitting logic into multiple nodes ensures modularity and simpler debugging.

A.15 Parameter

- **Definition**: A **configuration value** (like max speed, sensor thresholds) stored in a node, often loaded from YAML.

- **Analogy**: Like "tuning knobs" for your robot's behavior without editing code.

A.16 Publish/Subscribe

- **Definition**: The **unidirectional messaging** model in ROS2, where publishers send messages on a topic and subscribers receive them.

- **Benefit**: Decoupling—nodes don't need to know each other's existence explicitly.

A.17 QoS (Quality of Service)

- **Definition**: Settings that determine **reliability** (reliable vs. best-effort), **durability**, and other aspects of ROS2 data flow.

- **Example**: Reliable ensures every message is delivered, best-effort is faster but might drop messages.

A.18 Service

- **Definition**: A **request-response** mechanism in ROS2, used when a node needs an immediate reply from another node (like "open gripper" → "opened").

- **Analogy**: Like calling customer support—you ask, they respond.

A.19 SLAM (Simultaneous Localization and Mapping)

- **Definition**: The process of **building a map** of an unknown environment while **tracking** your location within it.

- **Use:** Key for robots in unfamiliar spaces or dynamic worlds (like a new building layout).

A.20 TF Tree

- **Definition:** The **network of coordinate frames** in tf2, showing how each link or sensor frames relate.

- **Why:** A consistent TF tree is vital for sensor fusion, navigation, and robot modeling.

Appendix B: Additional Python Resources and Tutorials

Python's **simplicity** and **powerful libraries** make it a natural fit for robotics. Below are recommended resources and tutorials for **refining** your Python skills, especially if you plan to integrate advanced **machine learning** or manage complex data pipelines within your ROS2 project.

B.1 Official Python Documentation

- **URL:** https://docs.python.org

- **Focus:** Comprehensive reference for the standard library, from basic syntax to modules like asyncio or multiprocessing.

Rhetorical Question: Ever find yourself uncertain about string methods or date/time manipulations? The official docs are your go-to.

B.2 Python for Robotics Tutorials

1. **OpenCV with Python**

   - o **What:** Basic image processing, color detection, shape recognition.

   - o **Why:** Often a first step to incorporating computer vision into your robot.

   - o **Resource:** PyImageSearch blog, official OpenCV docs.

2. **Machine Learning in Python**

   - o **SciKit-Learn:** For simpler classification, regression tasks.

   - o **TensorFlow / PyTorch:** For deep learning, neural network-based approaches.

   - o **Resource:** Coursera ML courses, fast.ai for deep learning on images.

ROS2 Python Tutorials

- o **Beginner:** Launching a Python node, publishing/subscribing, writing a service.

- o **Intermediate:** Parameter usage, dynamic reconfigure, advanced debugging.

- o **Advanced:** Action servers/clients, real-time Python with micro-ROS?

B.3 Interactive Environments and Online Tools

- **Jupyter Notebooks**: Quick prototyping, especially for data analysis or ML tasks.

- **Google Colab**: Free GPU support for deep learning experiments, though integration with local hardware might be limited.

- **VS Code Remote**: Connect your VS Code to a dev board (like a Raspberry Pi), allowing direct coding and debugging of your robot.

Appendix C: Recommended Tools, Libraries, and Hardware Vendors

This appendix shines a light on **practical resources**—the stuff you might actually buy or download. While not exhaustive, it's curated to reflect widely used, **reliable** options in the robotics community.

C.1 Development Boards and Single-Board Computers (SBCs)

1. **Raspberry Pi**

   - **Pros**: Affordable, active community, broad ecosystem.

   - **Ideal For**: Small to medium robots, educational prototypes.

   - **Vendors**: Pimoroni, Adafruit, Element14.

2. **NVIDIA Jetson Series**

   o **Pros:** Built-in GPU for real-time AI tasks.

   o **Ideal For:** Computer vision, deep learning on the edge.

   o **Vendors:** Official NVIDIA store, major electronics retailers.

3. **Intel NUC**

   o **Pros:** More powerful CPU/GPU combos, can handle heavier software workloads.

   o **Ideal For:** Larger robots, advanced autonomy with ROS2.

   o **Vendors:** Intel official site, Amazon, Newegg.

C.2 Sensors and Actuators

1. **LIDAR**

   o **Brands:** Hokuyo (compact, reliable), YDLIDAR (affordable), RPLIDAR (entry-level).

   o **ROS2 Drivers:** Usually provided by vendor or open-source community.

2. **Cameras**

   o **Brands:** Logitech (USB webcams), Intel RealSense (depth cameras), Basler (industrial).

- o **Use:** Vision-based SLAM, object detection, telepresence.

3. **Motors**

- o **DC Geared Motors:** Pololu, DFRobot.

- o **Servo Motors:** Dynamixel (smart servos with integrated feedback).

- o **Brushless:** T-Motor, EMAX (common in drones).

4. **IMUs**

- o **Vendors:** Bosch (BNO055), SparkFun (MPU-9250 modules), Adafruit.

- o **Integration:** Check for existing ROS2 drivers or ready-to-use Python libraries.

C.3 Libraries for Robotics

1. **OpenCV** (Computer Vision)

- o Real-time image processing, robust community support.

2. **PCL (Point Cloud Library)**

- o 3D processing, used for advanced object recognition with LIDAR or depth sensors.

3. **MoveIt!**

- o For manipulating robotic arms, collision checking, path planning (integrates well with ROS2).

C.4 Robotics Kits and Chassis Vendors

1. **TurtleBot Series**

    - o **Pros**: Official ROS support, well-documented, good for research or advanced hobby.

    - o **Vendor**: TurtleBot3 from ROBOTIS.

2. **DFRobot / Seeed Studio**

    - o Provide low-cost chassis, motor drivers, sensor kits for educational or small-scale projects.

3. **Nexus Robot**

    - o Omni-directional wheels and advanced chassis kits for holonomic drive robots.

Appendix D: Troubleshooting Reference Cheat Sheets

Even seasoned roboticists occasionally forget **common commands** or best practices. This **cheat sheet** collection condenses essential tips, focusing on **quick look-ups** during stressful debugging sessions. Keep them pinned on your lab wall or bookmarked on your dev machine.

D.1 ROS2 CLI Commands (Minimal Crash Course)

1. **Topic Management**

   o ros2 topic list: List all topics.

   o ros2 topic echo /topic_name: Print messages from /topic_name.

   o ros2 topic pub /topic_name std_msgs/msg/String "{data: 'hello'}": Publish a test message.

2. **Node Management**

   o ros2 node list: See running nodes.

   o ros2 node info <node_name>: Inspect node subscriptions/publications.

3. **Service Management**

   o ros2 service list: List active services.

   o ros2 service call /service_name std_srvs/srv/Empty: Call a service with an empty request.

4. **Action Management** (if installed)

   o ros2 action list: Display active actions.

   o ros2 action send_goal /navigate_to_pose nav2_msgs/action/NavigateToPose "{...}": Test sending a navigation goal.

D.2 Common QoS Settings

QoS Profile	Meaning
Reliable	Guarantee delivery of messages.
BestEffort	Faster, but may drop messages.
TransientLocal	Store messages for new subscribers.
KeepLast(n)	Store only the last n messages.

Tip: Mismatched QoS across a publisher and subscriber = no communication. Check or unify QoS profiles.

D.3 Parameter Quick Reference

- **List Node Parameters**: ros2 param list /node_name

- **Get Specific Param**: ros2 param get /node_name param_name

- **Set Param**: ros2 param set /node_name param_name value

D.4 RViz Visualization Hints

1. **Fixed Frame**: Typically map or odom, must be correct for data to appear in the right coordinate space.

2. **Add** → "By Topic" can auto-create correct display types for your messages.

3. **Camera** or **Image** displays: Confirm the image topic matches your camera's published topic.

4. **TF** display: Shows transforms. If frames appear disconnected, check your robot's URDF or tf2 broadcaster nodes.

D.5 Gazebo Simulation Gotchas

1. **Missing Plugins**: If you spawn a robot but nothing moves, confirm the gazebo_ros plugins are defined in URDF or SDF.

2. **Scaling Issues**: A small mismatch in model scale can cause collisions or odd physics. Check the <mass>, <inertia>, and <collision> tags.

3. **Slow Performance**: If your PC lags, reduce the **update rate**, **physics resolution**, or use a headless mode (gzserver without gzclient).

D.6 "What Next?" If All Else Fails

1. **Search**: The ROS2 Discourse forum or relevant GitHub repos for known issues.

2. **Ask**: Post a question with a clear summary of your environment, steps tried, and logs.

3. **Revert**: Roll back recent changes to isolate the cause.

4. **Take a Break**: Sometimes stepping away to clear your mind offers fresh insight (seriously).

Chapter Summary

These **Appendices** serve as a final, easily referenced toolkit to **amplify** your robotics journey with ROS2 and Python. Each section addresses a different set of needs:

1. **Appendix A**: Glossary of key concepts for quick recall—ideal for newcomers or anyone needing a refresher on robotics/ROS2 jargon.

2. **Appendix B**: Python resources, from official docs to machine learning tutorials, ensuring you can develop advanced scripts and AI solutions confidently.

3. **Appendix C**: Practical shopping list of recommended boards, sensors, software libraries, and chassis kits, linking real-world hardware and software to your ROS2 projects.

4. **Appendix D**: Troubleshooting cheat sheets and reference commands, perfect for **in-the-moment** debugging or short memory aids.

Use these appendices as your go-to reference when:

- You forget a command's syntax or the difference between certain QoS profiles.

- You need to find a new Python library for an advanced vision project.

- You're deciding which LIDAR or SBC is best for your next robot build.

- You run into unexpected simulation quirks or node connection issues.

By combining these resources with the **foundational** and **advanced** techniques learned throughout this book, you'll be well-equipped to solve real-world robotics challenges, from simple prototypes to large-scale deployments. **Stay curious—** the next wave of robotics breakthroughs might just come from your own creative experiments and unexpected mashups of these tools.